INWARD STILLNESS

by

GEORGE A. MALONEY, S.J.

DIMENSION BOOKS

DENVILLE, NEW JERSEY

Imprimi Potest: Rev. Eamon Taylor, S.J.
Provincial of New York Province
Sept. 15, 1975

Published by Dimension Books, Inc.
Denville, New Jersey 07834

– Dedication –

To my only sister, Joyce Elaine

ACKNOWLEDGMENTS

Grateful acknowledgment is made to the following publishers who have so generously granted permission to reprint from their publications: Darton, Longman & Todd, Ltd. and Doubleday & Company, Inc., N.Y. for excerpts from *The Jerusalem Bible,* copyright 1966 by Darton, Longman & Todd, Ltd. and Doubleday & Company, Inc. All scriptural texts are from *The Jerusalem Bible,* unless otherwise noted. Used by permission material found in my article that appeared under the title: "Tears and Enlightenment," in: *Review for Religious* (St. Louis, Feb. 1975) pp. 1397-1404. Also the use of material that appeared in my leaflet and pamphlet entitled: "Prayer of the Heart" published by Dove Publications (Pecos, N.M., 1973).

Finally great gratitude to my secretary, Mrs. Ann Kemble, for typing this manuscript.

TABLE OF CONTENTS

INTRODUCTION

In all of us there lies embedded deep down a drive towards communication. We want to say "I" to another. We wait eagerly for that other to say "you." Only 30% of human communication is done through human speech. The rest is accomplished through "body-talk": a touch, a smile, a frown, fire in the eyes, tightened shoulders; or through a mysterious alchemy of body-soul-spirit pulsation that conveys to a sensitive person volumes of messages not deciphered by the "outsider."

The songwriter, Bob Dylan, gives us a modern parable that expresses quite well what I wish to say. On the back side of his album, "John Wesley Harding" we read of three kings who visit a man named Frank. The first king explains their mission to Frank. "Mr. Dylan has come out with a new record. This record of course features none but his own songs and we understand that you're the key." "That's right," said Frank, "I am." "Well then," said the king in a bit of excitement, "could you please open it up for us?"

Frank, who all this time had been reclining with his eyes closed, suddenly opened them both up as wide as a tiger. "And just how far would you like to go in?" he asked. The chief of the kings replies: "Not too far but just enough so we can say that we've been there."

Many of us desire to learn the most mysterious art of communicating with God. But it is a mystery and our unraveling of God's mystery and ultimately our own lies in our readiness "to go in." Jesus Christ still asks the modern world, you and me: "and just how far would you like to go in?"

This book is an attempt to encourage the reader to go in, deeply, into your heart. The biblical concept of *heart* is used to designate that inner world of immanence in each person where God wishes to communicate with us in a language of love that has to be experienced beyond words, concepts, images or even emotional feelings. Most of us stand hesitatingly at the entrance of the cave of our heart. We really would like to go in. We suspect there is more to life, to God, to ourselves than our grasp of the mystery has up until now revealed to us. Some of us are ready to move more deeply in, but are more anxious to tell the world that we've been there, just a bit!

It's not easy to "let go" and live in mystery. There is so much darkness and insecurity. Shadows and snarling animals assail us on our journey. We hunger and thirst. We lose our way. We come close to perishing. God, why did I ever start! The Israelites got so far into the mystery and then wanted out, fast. "Back to Egypt, let's go," they cried out to Moses. There at least was security, even if it was slavery. But this desert pilgrimage is so hard! There's such stillness. Death is always close at hand. We feel so weak and poor.

"Inward Stillness" is an invitation to accept God's call: "Be still and know that I am God" (Ps. 46:10). These pages outline the mystery of deeper communication with God. I have sought to take the insights from the Eastern Christian writers on what they termed "the prayer of the heart" and develop them into a modern synthesis of Christian transcendental prayer.

Many Christians have reached an impasse in their prayer life. They would like to go deeper, but they fear moving into the unknown. Some Christians fear opening up the unconscious to the healing presence of Jesus Christ and suspect any deep, silent prayer as a form of "occultism" or at least of quietism. Others, dissatisfied with the impersonalized ritualism and dogmatism in certain Christian Churches, have turned to the Far East for inspiration. In their haste for "quick mysticism," "instant satori," they take one of two routes. For some, a new exotic world opens up of chanting, macrobiotics, incense, Sanscrit words and koans which takes them into a counter-culture that becomes an unreal world of make-believe.

For others they become deeply devoted to a disciplined method of meditation and put themselves completely under the guidance of a "guru." This type usually deserts Christianity or renders it so all embracing that a new religion develops for them, far removed from the historical Jesus and the Church's teaching of His message. These learn to empty their mind. But not rooted in a Christian community and the Church's traditions, they run the risk of exposing their deep psyche to demonic powers.

Yet how few Christians are well acquainted with a most authentic Christian mysticism in the form of Eastern Christian prayer of the heart. I have therefore tried in these pages to introduce readers to this form of prayer. It can be represented as a Christian form of transcendental meditation. I am not interested in doing a scientific comparison between Eastern Christian prayer of the heart and a modern course in Transcendental Meditation.

I am concerned more positively to explore the riches
of the Christian Eastern spirituality and to demythologize
what no longer serves as a cultural carrier of this universal
Christian experience of the indwelling God. I have striven
to use insights also from the Far East as well as from
modern psychology and the whole area of expanded
consciousness to present a form of deep interior prayer
that can lead us into God's mystery and make us better
human beings. If the reader is helped in any small way
along this path, the author will know he has accomplished
the scope of this book.

George A. Maloney, S.J.

1

The Silence of God

Modern man knows the silence of God. He stands on a craggy precipice overlooking an abyss and raises his finger to the heavens. "God, speak to me in my need! Where are You when I call on You? What am I to do, God? What way shall I take?" And there is silence! Man has all too often experienced the absence of God in his own inability to pierce the heavens and establish communication with the Absolute.

But God's true silence issues from His perfection and holiness. God is love and silence is the perfect communication of the Father and His Son through the Holy Spirit. Love needs no language, but it does express itself in perfect silence. God needs no multiplicity and variety to express His eternal continuity in love. He loves through His One Word. His silence is not broken by speaking His Word. His Word issues forth eternally in silence.

We punctuate our words with silence because we need to reflect, search out further ideas, correct or amplify what has just been said. God speaks continually His unchanging Word. He never utters a second or a third because in His Word He expresses perfectly all that He is.

9

God's Word, spoken from all eternity, is spoken perfectly. God could not improve by repeating Himself, as St. Paul declares, "because God wanted all perfection to be found in Him and all things to be reconciled through Him and for Him, everything in Heaven and everything on earth. . ." (Col. 1:19-20). And again St. Paul says: "In Him lives the fullness of divinity" (Col. 2:9).

God not only speaks His Word that flows from within the Father as the very expressed meaning of His eternal mind, but this interior Word, spoken from all eternity without interruption, is also heard by the Father as a perfect echo of His own reflected beauty. Speaking the Word in eternal silence through His outpouring Love that is His Holy Spirit, the Heavenly Father hears His Word come back to Him in a perfect, eternal, "yes" of total, surrendering Love, that is again the Holy Spirit.

The theological controversy between the Orthodox and Catholic Churches about the *Filioque* (whether the Holy Spirit proceeds from the Father alone or also from the Son) is no controversy when contemplated in the eternal begetting of God's Word in God's Love. Both Churches hold a partial statement of the truth. The contemplative who stands before this sacred mystery knows in a knowledge given only by God's Spirit that the Holy Spirit proceeds as Love from the Father and in that same proceeding act of Love the Word is eternally spoken. But the Son echoes this Divine Love as He, the Word, goes back to the Father in the same Divine Spirit. The Spirit originates from the Father, but He proceeds back to the Father as the Word's loving response.

The contemplative, experiencing the triadic movement of Love from Father to Son and Son back to the Father, experiences also the profound silence of the Holy

Spirit. The Word is *spoken*. The Holy Spirit is not the Word spoken. He is the deepest expression of love uttered in ecstatic silence! God the Father has said everything in His one Word. Love pours itself out in the silence of one Word uttered. But Divine Love also is the silence of repose in which the Word freely comes back to rest in the eternal embrace of His Father. "He who sent me is with me and has not left me to myself, for I always do what pleases Him" (Jn. 8:29).

To those who have deeply loved, God's repose, His gaze of love, the peaceful fulfillment of all His desires in His Word will be easily understood as the Holy Spirit's silent gasp of mutual, loving surrender.

Bossuet has a beautiful sermon in which he struggles to express this mystery of the interrelationship of Father, Son and Holy Spirit:

> Remember that in God there are only two processions by which all is produced within Himself: that of the Word and that of the Holy Spirit; in the first one He speaks and brings forth His only Son; in the other one He does not speak, but He sighs and brings forth from His heart, that is from His will, His divine Love, which we call His Spirit; and this adorable Spirit is the end and the perfection of everything that is being accomplished in God.

GOD'S SILENCE IN CREATION

Through God's one Word, all of creation is brought forth into existence. Mountains and oceans, birds and beasts, flowers and grains tumble forth in profuse richness from the finger tips of the creating God.

Yes, as the rain and snow come down from the heavens and do not return without watering the earth, making it yield and giving growth to provide seed for the sower and bread for the eating, so the Word that goes from My mouth does not return to Me empty, without carrying out My will and succeeding in what it was sent to do. (Is. 55:10-11).

St. John tells us that through God's Word that was with Him in the beginning in silence before there was any multiplied creation all things were made. "Through Him all things came to be, not one thing had its being but through Him" (Jn. 1:3). The Israelites in the words of the Psalmist clearly grasped God's creative force in His Word:

By the word of Yahweh the heavens were made,
their whole array by the breath of His mouth,
He collects the ocean waters as though in a wineskin,
He stores the deeps in cellars (Ps. 33:6).

St. Irenaeus in the second century describes God as bringing forth the created world through His two hands — His Divine Word and the Holy Spirit. Not only does God create the whole material world in the silence of His Word and His Spirit of Love, but He holds them in being also in silence. He brings them to completion in the silence of millions of years of unfolding, pent-up powers locked in the seeds of His first creation. God is an Evolver and He evolves His material world in silence.

He whispers through the dark and empty void: "Let there be light" (Gen. 1:3) and there was light. "Let there be a vault in the waters to divide the waters in two" (Gen. 1:6). "Let the waters under heaven come together. . . .let dry land appear" (Gen. 1:9-10). "Let the earth produce vegetation" (Gen. 1:11). God's creative speech unfolds in silence through the aeons of time necessary for His Word and His Spirit to bring all things into their fullness.

But when God's creative energy fashions man as His *chef-d'oeuvre*, He turns within Himself and the *I* of God speaks to the *We* within and in that loving silence says: "Let us make man in Our own image, in the likeness of Ourselves" (Gen. 1:26).

In a perceptive text of the Midrash, it is written:

> And Isaac asked the Eternal: 'King of the World, when Thou didst make the light, Thou didst say in Thy Torah that the light was good; when Thou didst make the extent of the firmament and the extent of the earth, Thou didst say in Thy Torah that they were good; but when Thou hadst made man in Thine image, Thou didst not say in Thy Torah that man was good. Wherefore Lord?' And God answered him, 'Because man I have not yet perfected, and because through the Torah man is to perfect himself, and to perfect the world.'[1]

Of all God's creatures spoken in the silence of His Creative Word and His loving Spirit, man alone is perfectible by answering *yes* to God's call to share in His silent love. Only man in prayer can be aware of being personally loved by God. Only in prayer he alone can return that love as in a godly silence he stills his own desires, plans, ideas of God, himself and his world that he is constantly seeking to create according to his own desires and returns through God's Word and His Holy Spirit to his Heavenly Father.

Bossuet again speaks of God's creation of things and finally of man. He shows man's greatest dignity to consist in having a soul that is the breath of God, the sigh of God's heart, the Holy Spirit, breathed into man to make him a uniquely living spirit-to-Spirit relationship.

God has likewise created all things in a twofold manner: by speaking and by breathing. He first created all the beings of our immense universe by speaking: 'Fiat lux, fiat firmamentum,' and, when after all that he came to the creation of our soul, He did not speak. He sighed. Holy Scripture says that the creation of the human soul is the last of God's work in creation, the end and perfection of His works outside Himself, and that He rested as though in contemplation of so beautiful a work.

What soul, ignorant though it may be, would not be overcome with joy at considering the awe-inspiring likeness and the wonderful relation that God has deigned to establish between His Spirit and our spirit? The Holy Spirit is a silent Sigh in the heart of God. And in this Spirit God finds an infinite joy and delight within Himself. Our soul is also a breath, a sigh from the heart of God and in it God takes great pleasure outside of Himself. The Holy Spirit is the last of the works of God within Himself and our soul is the last of all the works of God outside of Himself. O God of love, to what raptures of joy would not this truth carry us if we really let it sink into our souls, if we could really understand it! How can anyone help exclaiming with St. Augustine and St. Bernard: 'O my soul, you have the glory of bearing the image of God, you have received this greatest honor of being a spirit from God, of being a sigh from His heart so full of love and goodness for us. Should you not love this God of Goodness who has loved you so much? Love Him alone, love Him ardently and be consumed by the flames of His divine love. Amen.

GOD SPEAKS TO NATURE IN SILENCE

Most of us have learned from time to time in our busy lives to turn aside from man's manipulated world and to come in contact again with God's primeval presence in nature. An unforgetable, peak experience in my life was to stand on the roof of St. Catherine's Monastery at the foot of Mt. Sinai in the evening and experience God's immense silent presence in the stars and galaxies that burst over my head, seeming so close to me that I found myself reaching out as though to touch them, the flaming loving eyes of God of the desert! It was probably at such a time that Pascal cried out: "The eternal silence of those boundless spaces strikes awe into my soul."

In touch with God's silence found in unspoiled nature, man begins to become a contemplative. He admires God's beauty and harmony in nature and prays with St. Augustine:

> Heaven and earth and all that is in the universe cry out to me from all directions that I, O God, must love THEE, and they do not cease to cry out to all so that they have no excuse.

The inanimate world is filled with a natural silence. Rocks and mountains have stood sentinel at the gate that says: "Leave all noise behind. Be silent and know I am your God."

God pulsates with His silent energies in all of animate nature, plants, trees, birds and animals, that cry out unceasingly to the noisy pilgrims on the roadside, ". . .in Him we live and move and exist" (Acts 17:28).

How silently a giant sequoia grows over centuries, stretching its head towards its Maker in praise and adoration. The butterfly moves about in its beautiful silence telling us humans of the God of silence.

> Yahweh, what variety you have created,
> Arranging everything so wisely!
> Earth is completely full of things
> You have made (Ps. 104:24).

All things in nature, animate and inanimate, function in harmony with a minimum of friction, conflict and noise. A. Gehlen tells the story of an Indian boy and girl from British Columbia going into the forest and fasting in order to learn the language of owls.[2] Siddhartha in Hermann Hesse's novel learned the secret of life by listening to the ancient but ever new river speak to him. The American Indian can sit for hours and not waste time but be fully active in his communion with his true self, i.e. himself in relationship with the oneness of the whole created world around him that is speaking to his deepest self about his Maker in the silence of nature.

The man of silent prayer who has learned to enter into his heart is similar to the primitive man insofar as both develop through the silencing of their discursive powers a keen sense of the cosmic unity among all creatures.

We see a difference in the non-technological world's concept of time and music. The daily, monthly, yearly cycles are built up through a sense of passing particulars through changes of light and darkness by the movement of the silent sun, moon, stars and earth. Music from the East, including the Eastern Christian world, is basically a melody and rhythm with no mathematical harmony or counterpoint. The "drone" gives the reality of cyclical timelessness that roots man in the presence of something eternal and unchangeable, through which the peripheral and the changeable pass.[3]

Touching God's silence in all of nature changes also one's approach to ethical values. The concept of good is not so much doing good, ethical acts that conform to a pre-existent norm, but rather is based on being immersed in and sensitive to the inner harmony in all of nature. The

Chinese called it living according to the Tao or the Ying and Yang found in all things. In such a society the law of status is important and justice is obtained not by law and force but through an ethics of mediation or listening.

Modern man needs to turn into his "heart" and in silence, he must enter deeply into himself and hear his true Self, the Absolute Ground of all being tell him through experiential knowledge, through enlightenment, that the world of senses is not the totality of reality, but through an experience man understands that he is one with all being.

Man needs to quiet his reasoning powers, which is not the same as to let them atrophy. Man is noisily planning his world in his mind but he lacks the cosmic blueprint. In such prayerful communion with God in the silence of nature, man can learn to approach the whole of reality and let it be without the nervous "will to power" of Nietzsche, to change and convert it into something new according to his own conceptualization. Man introduces his "noise" and lack of harmony into the silence of God's nature. Western man's mind is constantly chattering noisily about an abstract world. Meanwhile the real world gets farther and farther away from man making man an exile on this earth, an enemy of nature and of God. We have lost the wonderment of children who can enjoy simple reality with a curiosity and openness that allows them *to be* there, rather than wanting always *to do* something. We live in the mind, disregarding the body. We have forgotten the simple rhythm that God has planted within all of us that is one with the silent rhythm found in all of nature, especially found in the beauties of nature, inanimate and animate.

Such a child of God, filled with God's silence in His beauties of nature can appreciate the depths of Gerard Manley Hopkins *God's Grandeur*:

The world is charged with the grandeur of God.
It will flame out, like shining from shook foil;
    It gathers to a greatness, like the ooze of oil
Crushed. Why do men then now not reck his rod?
Generations have trod, have trod, have trod;
    And all is seared with trade; bleared, smeared
      with toil;
    And wears man's smudge and shares man's smell;
      the soil
Is bare now, nor can foot feel, being shod.

And for all this, nature is never spent;
    There lives the dearest freshness deep down things;
And though the last lights off the black West went
Oh, morning, at the brown brink eastward, springs —
Because the Holy Ghost over the bent
    World broods with warm breast and with ah'
      bright wings.

GOD'S SILENCE IN MAN

But God's silence grows deeper and more intense when He communicates with man, made according to His own image and likeness. God's silence in all of nature flows from His infinite love for man. Therefore as He gives Himself more directly to man in the depths of man's being, in his heart, God does so in the silence of begetting His Word through the fiery gaze of the Spirit of Love.

It is in silence that the Christian learns as Moses to stand before the Burning Bush. Man finds his greatest struggle in becoming silent before God's silent love. It entails a letting go of the control man has over his life. It is a death to his false life in order to find his true life in the Other dwelling intimately within him.

Nikos Kazantzakis describes this decision to yield to God: "God is fire and you must walk on it. . .dance on it. At that moment the fire will become cool water. But until you reach that point, what a struggle, my Lord, what agony!"

It is the struggle in faith to accept the silent love of the indwelling God. St. Augustine exhorts us: "Enter into yourself; it is in the interior man where Truth is found." When man in silence hears God's silence through faith, he comes into the presence of a dynamic God, acting and loving within man. God is accomplishing in the secret of his heart His great work of divinizing love.

It is the Holy Spirit that reveals the light of God's inner love. He gives man interior ears to comprehend what God's silence is saying. He brings forth in man as the fruit of this triadic love peace that flows from the limpid confidence man, the child of Abba, Father, shows toward Him in all circumstances of his life, beginning in the silent darkness of his heart. As he sees the demonic swirlings of haunting memories rise up from within him, he surrenders to his Father in absolute submission. He cries out for healing and new life.

The external events of his life also unfold before the backdrop of God's loving silence as Father. Man radiates a peace and serenity towards others that is recognized by all as joy. Only the Christian who has experienced in deep silence God's great love and knows with the certitude of experience given by God's Spirit that he is loved by the Holy of Holies can afford to be always joyful and rejoicing.

GOD IS SILENT LOVE

We have seen how God is silent within Himself. The Begetter and the Begotten and the unifying Love between Them are relationships of loving presence that unfold in silence.

God creates and sustains the universe of inanimate and animate creatures in His silent "in-presence" to each being that He holds in existence in His silently spoken Word.

But man alone of all creatures is able by faith to "hear" God's silent love breathing within himself. He alone is a temple of God being constantly begotten a child of God by the Uncreated Triadic Energies within him. St. Ignatius of Antioch grasped the silence of God and the necessity for man to be silent in listening to God's Word. He writes to the Ephesians:

> Anyone who is really possessed of the word of Jesus can listen to His silence and so be perfect; so that he may act through his words and be known by his silence.[4]

We need to develop at greater length the silence of man within his heart that God may bring forth His Word. Only then can we begin to understand what it should mean that a Christian should pray always in his heart. We will learn that the prayer of the heart is really the constant prayer of the Holy Spirit within us.

2

A Silenced Heart

Mount Athos, the Holy Mountain inhabited by Orthodox Monks, is a peninsula which juts out about 35 miles from northern Greece into the clear, shimmering waters of the Aegean Sea. It receives its name from the actual peak called Mount Athos which rises like an inverted cone domineering over woods spangled with monasteries and hermits' huts and wrapped usually in cotton-candied clouds of fog.

I have had the privilege of spending three summers living with these Orthodox monks in their theocratic republic that is totally closed to women. Most monks have adamantly resisted the "world" of cars, electricity, radios and newspapers. It is still a rugged, primitive society of men dedicated to the interior life and to silence. After doing my doctoral studies on the Fathers of the desert and the ancient hesychastic tradition, I wanted to profit for my own spiritual life from these monks who perpetuated this ancient Eastern Christian spirituality. I especially wanted to visit Karoulia, the southernmost tip of Mt. Athos where a small group of monks still live in little hermitages or huts that stand precariously on the rocky precipice, staring defiantly at the deep, swirling waters 250 feet below.

I had studied the writings of the Fathers in the *Apophthegmata Patrum*, the *Life of St. Anthony*, Macarius' homilies, the writings of Evagrius of Pontus, John Climacus in his *Thirty Steps*, Symeon the New Theologian and the writings on the Jesus Prayer collected in *Philokalia*, the special collection of hesychastic writings. But being a pragmatic American, I kept asking myself: "Does this ancient Christian spirituality have anything to tell the modern world?" At Karoulia I found the exact asceticism that had been practised in the 4th and 5th centuries in Egypt and Syria when the deserts became a "thebaid" of monks. Thousands of them fled the pagan world so that they could live literally the Gospel in all its stark simplicity. Here was the same approach. But where was the world? If their spirituality could not even withstand a look upon a beautiful woman, a newsbroad-cast of war from a radio, of what use other than a museum piece was all of that?

One of the great difficulties in transporting some language, practices, doctrine from the past to the present time is that, in the words of Dr. John Macquarrie,[1] "coherence" is lost. Reading words from the writings of the Fathers of the desert such as *heart, world, tranquillity, guarding the thoughts*, could lead us into a language of total irrelevance for us in the 20th century. We can then in disgust dismiss the wisdom of such early mystics as "not really with it" and go on our way to discover truth for ourselves. Man tends to be the same throughout all generations. He has a built-in hunger to meet God both within the depths fo his being as well as in his being *there*, right in the heart of his real, contemporary world (Heidegger's *Da-sein*).

Man has always sought in myths and legends, much as we see in the Genesis "myth" of the creation of the world and of man by God, man's sinfulness and rebellion against God. The deeper man probes to find insights in regard to his ultimate destiny, the more he must turn to mythopoetic language. We are no exception in this matter. Yet it was Carl G. Jung who lamented the fact that Western man had become impoverished in his use of symbols to transcend his horizontal optic in order to make contact with the Ultimate Ground of his being.

I do not want to present this book as a historical re-presentation of what the Fathers of the desert said about the spiritual life. I would like to spring from some of the insights of such early Eastern Christian mystics to insights that might be still most applicable for us moderns, without at the same time merely reproducing the same language. I would like to get inside of the "reality" that such early saints wrote about because they had so deeply experienced what they wrote about. The same "reality" should be equally meaningful for all of us.

THE HEART

Hesychasm refers to that type of Eastern Christian spirituality that has its roots in the Fathers of the desert who strove through constant custody of the "heart" and continual prayer to experience the divinization of man into a "new creature," a child of God, by grace. It comes from the Greek word, *hesychia*, which means tranquillity or quietude. Built upon a rigorous asceticism of constant control of one's thoughts by vigilant attention to the presence of the indwelling God, fasting, cultivation of *penthos*, which is an abiding sense of sorrow for sin, it

centered its prayer life chiefly around the monological
prayer called the Jesus Prayer: "Lord, Jesus Christ, Son of
God, have mercy on me a sinner."

It is an ancient spirituality that flows out of the
scriptural use of "heart" to mean the inner core of man's
being, the "focus" where man enters to meet the Transcendent God, as immanently present and divinizing man
"according to God's image and likeness" (Gen. 1:26). In
the words of St. Gregory of Sinai of the 14th century, man
stands before God in prayer, with concentration by the
grace of faith in the indwelling Trinity and "forces his
mind into his heart." The goal of such spirituality is not to
reach a religious "high," to have an ecstatic experience. It
is to fulfill the injunction of the New Testament, to pray
always. It is to be re-created into the fullness of matured
sons of God.

More primarily, it is "to let go" of one's creaturely
hold on his own life to enter into a conscious relationship
with God as not only Creator but above all as loving
Father and to live each moment in the light of that
relationship. From the earliest Christian tradition, man has
been encouraged to stretch forth to attain an ever greater
awareness, constancy and honesty in his relationship with
God. Cassian summarizes the whole of the Christian life as
attaining "purity of heart."

In Holy Scripture we see that *heart* is more than the
physical organ that is the center of our bodily life. The
central command of Judaism and Christianity: "You shall
love Yahweh your God with all your heart, with all your
soul, with all your strength" (Deut. 6:5) indicates that
heart means more than just the seat of emotions. It is the
center of man's spirit where man can communicate and
surrender himself totally in love to God. It is the "place"

where I take my life in hand and fashion it for good or evil into what I wish myself to become. God says: "Give me your heart" (Prov. 23:26) which is God's plea for a total commitment and a total surrender in loving service to God as man's Master and Lord.

The Lord is able to know man's deepest being; He reads man's heart. "God does not see as man sees; man looks at appearances but Yahweh looks at the heart" (1 Sam. 16:7). He searches every heart and knows every plan that man devises (1 Chron. 28:9). The heart therefore is a powerful, primeval "myth" that Holy Scripture uses to describe that, beyond the constitutive parts of man as a bodied, soul, spirited being, he possesses a center of deliberation, of free choice whereby man can determine his ontological stance before God.

Evil as well as good proceeds from the heart. "For out of the heart proceeds evil reasoning, murder, adultery, fornication, theft, lying, blasphemy..." (Matt. 15:19). Yet only the pure of heart will see God (Matt. 5:8). The heart needs cleansing from within and then the vessel will also be clean on the outside (Matt. 23:26). Man believes in his heart and in his heart he meets his Savior and is made righteous. St. Paul tells us:

> If your lips confess that Jesus is Lord and if you believe in your heart that God raised Him from the dead, then you will be saved. By believing from the heart you are made righteous; by confessing with your lips you are saved (Rom. 10:9).

Jesus Christ came to teach us that we were to adore our Heavenly Father not just by our lips but in our hearts, that is, on the deepest level of our personality, where we could consciously surrender ourselves to His controlling

will. Beyond the impulsiveness of our sense life, our
emotions and intellectual formation, there lies the heart,
the secret, inner recess wherein the Holy Spirit dwells and
prays for us in our inability to pray to the Father as we
ought.

> The Spirit too comes to help us in our weakness. For when we
> cannot choose words in order to pray properly, the Spirit
> Himself expresses our plea in a way that could never be put
> into words, and God who knows everything in our *hearts*
> knows perfectly well what He means, and that the pleas of the
> saints expressed by the Spirit are according to the mind of
> God (Rom. 8:26-27).

MAN'S CENTER

The heart therefore is the center of man's being, that
which directs man in his ultimate values and choices. It
is the inner chamber where in secret the Heavenly Father
sees man through and through. St. Theophan the Recluse
(1815-1894) describes the heart in the hesychastic tradition as not only the material heart, the central organism
that pumps life-giving blood into the whole body but:

> The heart is the innermost man, or spirit. Here are located
> self-awareness, the conscience, the idea of God and of one's
> complete dependence on Him, and all the eternal treasures of
> the spiritual life...Where is the heart? Where sadness, joy,
> anger, and other emotions are felt, here is the heart. Stand
> there with attention. The physical heart is a piece of muscular
> flesh, but it is not the flesh that feels, but the soul; the carnal

heart serves as an instrument for these feelings, just as the brain serves as an instrument for the mind. Stand in the heart, with the faith that God is also there, but how He is there do not speculate. Pray and entreat that in due time love for God may stir within you by His grace.[2]

How can we understand the symbol of "heart" theologically? We do know that God is always and everywhere present. He stands at the door of man's heart or consciousness, ready to enter, if only man opens the door or becomes consciously aware of God's presence. Dr. J. Macquarrie helps us with his concept of "focus."[3] It is because of man's present condition in the world that God communicates Himself to man through symbols that partake of a quality of concreteness, of the world and of man's history in that world. In man's deepest relationship with God as an I-Thou relationship man's *I* is too diffused and abstract. It requires a focus in order that this relationship as a concretized presence may be discerned and hence become open to man's consciousness.

We find such a focus on God's part in the Incarnation. God's divine Word is "localized." His *Shekinah* which was localized in the Old Testament in the Ark of the Covenant and in the Holy of Holies of Solomon's Temple is now brought down to a concrete person, Jesus of Nazareth. "The Word was made flesh, He pitched His tent among us, and we saw His glory, the glory that is His as the only Son of the Father, full of grace and truth" (Jn. 1:14).[4] God is focused in another special way in man's encounter with the sacramental presence of Jesus Christ, especially in the Holy Eucharist.

THE HEART – MAN'S FOCUS ON GOD

In a similar way, man as a being-in-the-world needs to be focused. The heart is both a physical organ and a basic symbol of man's existence in life. Even more, the heart symbolizes man's transcendence beyond the world, of his inner stretching power within his spirit to go towards God in thought and love. The writers of Holy Scripture were using a powerful "myth" to give us a symbol of the focus point where man was existentially rooted in existence in this world and still where he could swing free from this world and move in spirit into the fullness of why he came into existence, namely, to embrace God in a loving relationship of son to Father. The Hesychastic Fathers were only being scriptural when they used the heart as the place where man encounters God both with his existential self that at times needs healing from God and with his transformed, gifted self as a "new creature" in Jesus Christ.

St. Macarius captures this double aspect of man's heart as the focus of meeting God in man's concrete existence, the result of his Sitz-im-Leben, and the divinizing effect of the holy Spirit working through grace to transcend man into a fully realized human, made according to the Image and Likeness that is Jesus Christ:

> Grace engraves the laws of the Spirit in the hearts of the sons of light. Therefore, they should not draw their assurances from the Holy Scriptures alone, but the grace of God also inscribes the laws of the Spirit and the heavenly mysteries on the tablets of the heart. For the heart commands and rules the whole body. And grace, once it has filled the heart, reigns over all our members and thoughts. For in the heart are the spirit and all

the thoughts of the soul and its hope. Through it, grace passes to all the members of the body. We become unlike the children of darkness in whose heart sin rules and from which sin infects the entire body.

Macarius goes on to insist that those who wish to approach the Lord should make their prayer in a state of calm (*hesychia*), peace and great tranquillity, without anxiety and confusion. "Rather let him come to the Lord with complete attention, with effort of the heart and sobriety of thought *(nepsis)*."

SILENCE

If man is to meet God deeply within his heart, he must learn to silence his heart. What a lost art is this, to silence our hearts! How agitated with thoughts, desires, fears, anxieties we are when we come before the Lord in prayer! The greater our "distraction" or diffusion, the less conscious is our prayer, the less unifying is our union of mind with the mind of God in a loving surrender. Western man especially is proned by his highly developed rational gifts through science towards a chattering mind. He finds it very difficult to "let go" and surrender to a God that must be encountered through faith that presents Him as darkly, as in a mirror (1 Cor. 13:12). He tends to be the master, sure of himself, afraid to step out beyond the controls of his senses and his scientific method.

Yet God says: "Be still, and know that I am God" (Ps. 46:10, KJV). God calls us into a silence of the heart where all artificiality crumbles, new psychic and spiritual powers burgeon forth, released through the uncreated

energies of God. Silence is the interior air that the spirit of
man needs in order to grow spiritually. Such silence leads
man into the inner recess and there his Heavenly Father
will recompense him (Matt. 6:6). This recompensing comes
to man in the healing of psychic disturbances, the chaotic
meaninglessness of so many past experiences that hang like
dried skeletons within man's memories, the anxieties that
force man into an isolation of deadly loneliness. Man
becomes consoled, loved by God in an experience that is
beyond concepts. He knows that he knows God loves him!
This being-loved-by-God experience at the deepest level of
his consciousness restores his strength, pushes him to new
self-giving and creativity.

Silence takes place on several levels just as heart is a
reality for man on various levels of meaning. Silence is the
heart on these levels moving toward total integration.
There is the silence on the physical level. Here man learns
to bring an exterior silence into his body, his speech, his
walk, his gestures, his general composure radiating a deep
centering interiorly. One cannot be centered deeply if he is
continually babbling without the control of weighing his
words, his thoughts before the indwelling God.

Today physical silence of the body, beyond mere
silence of speech, is becoming more difficult. For those
who have taught children in grade school or are parents,
the growing problem of over-stimulated children is becoming crucial in their lives. Many such children cannot
compose themselves long enough to focus their attention
over a span of five minutes in class or at home. Many find
difficulty in relaxing enough to fall asleep. The noisy
world outside arouses man and keeps his whole physical
body in a state of tension. Watch a student trying to
concentrate deeply while listening to ear-splitting rock
music! His whole body is noisy and agitated.

The Israelites were brought into the desert by God, uprooted from their habitual, enslaving surroundings of Egypt, the flesh pots, and brought into the silence of the desert. Moving from noise to silence is always an uprooting, a leaving of something for something else. Yet there cannot be any movement into the inner silencing of the heart unless there be a movement away from physical noise, whether that be from outside distracting noises or the distracting noises that we allow our bodies to produce when we are not centered. "Your salvation lay in conversion and tranquillity, your strength, in complete trust; and you would have none of it" (Isaias 30:15).

That conversion consists in an inward turning, to attain an interior silence of the soul, of all the mental activities of our interior faculties of memory, understanding and will. Many spiritual people have turned inwardly away from the noises of the physical world only to find deafening noises inside their minds. Great discipline of the mind is needed to uproot such noise and find that inner peace and tranquillity that can come only if man's mind is focused more deeply upon God as the inner fortress of his strength.

A GIFT OF THE HOLY SPIRIT

That deeper focus is the silence of the heart where we attain a childlike trust, joy and peace in the embrace of the indwelling God. This silence is a gift from God's Spirit. It flows as fruit from deep union with God outwardly to effect not only a deeper silence of the mind but a silence that affects also the very way we look at others, smile, the way we walk and talk. St. Paul described the fruit of such silence of the heart as: "...love, joy, peace, patience, kindness, goodness, trustfulness, gentleness and self-control. . . . You cannot belong to Christ Jesus unless you crucify all self-indulgent passions and desires" (Gal. 5:22-24). When the heart is silent and the whole man is integrated, then he enters into the Kingdom of Heaven that is within. He comes into his true nature, the manner of *being* to himself, to God, to others that God had always intended in creating him with spiritual powers to communicate with Himself.

St. Basil writes: "When the mind is no longer dissipated across the world through the senses, it returns to itself; and by means of itself it ascends to the thought of God." It is a call into the desert that is within us. That inner space is chaos until God's creative Spirit can hover over it and shed God's light within man's darkness. The light of the Word of God stirs man to inner freedom as Jesus Christ promised: "If you make My word your home, you will indeed be My disciples, you will learn the truth and the truth will make you free" (Jn. 8:31-32).

Inward silence comes from an inner solitude where we learn to leave the outside, flattering world of the senses and illusions and descend into our poverty. It can only come through a hunger and thirst for the transcendent that escapes the grasp of the senses. St. Isaac of Nineveh, one of the great Eastern Christian mystics of the 7th century, expresses this inner descent that becomes a true ascent to God:

> Be at peace with your own soul, then heaven and earth will be at peace with you. Enter eagerly into the treasure house that is within you, and so you will see the things that are in heaven; for there is but one single entry to them both. The ladder that leads to the Kingdom is hidden within your soul. Flee from

sin, dive into yourself, and in your soul you will discover the stairs by which to ascend.[5]

The Hesychastic Fathers were writing for monks, those specialized Christians who could afford literally to leave society, live a life of continued silence and solitude. The Abba Arsenius gave the norm for such solitaries when in prayer he heard a voice which said to him: "Arsenius, flee, keep silence, remain tranquil" (*Fuge, tace, quiesce*). These are the roots of impeccability.[6]

NEED FOR DAILY SILENCE

But for most humans today such a life is virtually impossible. Most of us are lucky to find a few days for an extended retreat during the year. And yet, our silence and solitude must be a living experience, some time during each day if we are to grow in the prayer of the heart. Such silence and solitude must be created in the heart some time in early morning before our day begins to unfold at its hectic pace and then again in the evening. It will be an interior desert that we must enter into daily. There we will learn to stand before God in honesty, humility, silent to our own powers to tell God what we have been doing for Him. It will be a period of stripping ourselves of all our artificial masks and rationalizations that we so easily hide behind during the day's activities. It will be a centering upon God as the Source of all our energies. Soon we will look forward to such moments of silence. The beginning fears of being alone with God will soon yield to a peace and even joy at "pulling" ourselves together before our Ultimate Concern. A strength comes over us equipping us for the day's work from focusing in utter silence upon God.

St. Gregory of Nyssa has well captured the value of turning within to pull oneself together by turning to God as center. He writes:

> Let us imagine a stream flowing from a spring and branching out at random into different channels. Now so long as it flows this way it will be entirely useless for the cultivation of the soul. Its waters are spread out too much; each single channel is small and meager, and the water, because of this, hardly moves. But if we could collect these wandering and widely scattered channels into one single stream, we would have a full and compact waterflow which would be useful for the many needs of life.

> So too, I think, it is with the human mind. If it spreads itself out in all directions, constantly flowing out and dispersing to whatever pleases the senses, it will never have any notable force in its progress towards the true Good. But now recall the mind from all sides, and make it collect itself, so that it may begin to operate in that function which is preferably connatural to it, without scattering and wasting itself: then the mind will find no obstacle in its rise to heaven and in its grasp of the true meaning of reality.[7]

We can easily enough see where the fault lies in not praying more deeply. It is because we avoid turning deeply within ourselves and remaining in silence. Our fragmented, sinful nature does not like to live in silence because silence has a way of revealing ourselves beyond all poses. We pray with distractions and without force because we are afraid to be ourselves. And we refuse to be ourselves by refusing to enter into silence in the depth of our hearts.

We have said this silence is more than mere physical silence of not speaking orally when in prayer. It is basically an inner state of humility and poverty. As the Spirit of God lets His light of truth shine upon our true selves, we are filled with a sense of not only our nothingness and sinfulness before the beauty of the All-Holy, but we become broken in spirit. No longer is there the cocky, self-assured human being who has been convinced that he has truly met the Lord in all his rationalization and action. He stands empty before the richness of God, a beggar with nothing to commend himself. "My sacrifice is this broken spirit. You will not scorn this crushed and broken heart" (Ps. 51:17). We realize God cannot be manipulated any longer by ourselves. He must be approached with fear and trembling. Poverty and silence coalesce before the awesome presence of the Lord that is revealed to the empty-hearted. Silence teaches us that God must reveal Himself to us and we must wait for Him to speak. "Speak, Yahweh, Your servant is listening" (1 Sam. 3:9). "Behold the handmaid of the Lord; be it unto me according to thy word" (Lk. 1:38; KJV).

THE PARADOX OF SILENCE

What seems to be living in light when we live on the surface of our being is really to live in darkness. When we withdraw from noise and our own control over our lives and enter into a waiting silence before God to speak His Word we truly make a transition from darkness to light. There comes to us a deeper awareness of hidden things. We begin to move freely into the inner world of the invisible. At first it seems to be our own weakness to comprehend

God and our true selves. But it becomes a realization as we persevere in silence that it is because of God's great transcendence living within us that fills us with an inner silence that becomes the most intense manner of man communicating with God.

Thomas Merton has captured the paradox of emptying silence that is a true filling up with the richness of God Himself in the following quotation:

All the paradoxes about the contemplative way are reduced to this one: being without desire means being led by a desire so great that it is incomprehensible. It is too huge to be completely felt. It is a blind desire, which seems like a desire for "nothing" only because nothing can content it. And because it is able to rest in no-thing, then it rests, relatively speaking, in emptiness. But not in emptiness as such, emptiness for its own sake. Actually there is no such entity as pure emptiness and the merely negative emptiness of the false contemplative is a "thing" not a "nothing." The "thing" that it is is simply the darkness of self, from which all other beings are deliberately and of set-purpose excluded.
But true emptiness is that which transcends all things, and yet is immanent in all. For what seems to be emptiness in this case is pure being. It is not this, not that. Whatever you say of it, it is other than what you say. The character of emptiness, at least for a Christian contemplative, is pure love, pure freedom. Love that is free of everything, not determined by any thing or held down by any special relationship. It is love for love's sake. It is a sharing, through the Holy Spirit, in the infinite charity of God. And so when Jesus told His disciples to love, He told them to love as universally as the Father who sends His rain alike on the just and the unjust. "Be ye perfect as Your Heavenly Father." This purity, freedom and indeterminateness of love is the very essence of Christianity. It is to this above all that monastic prayer aspires.[8]

Karl Rahner speaks of this inner silence moving out into our everyday life by which our most commonplace actions are grounded in and directed toward the mystery of God.

If we are silent, if we forgive, if without reward we give ourselves wholeheartedly and are detached from ourselves, we are reaching out into a limitlessness which exceeds any assignable bound and which is nameless. We are reaching out towards the holy mystery which pervades and is the ground of our life. We are dealing with God.[9]

Darkness and silence are the realms of the Father within the contemplative. He is the uncreated Ground of being, the abyss of mystery. But He speaks His Word that is light, revelation, speech and meaning to those who attune themselves to His silent speaking of that Word. Man must wait simply upon God's gratuitous gift of His Word spoken when man has surrendered himself in the silencing of all his own powers to become utter receptivity before God's mysterious gift of love. To understand this basic paradox of hearing in silence the Word spoken by God, of seeing by not seeing, of darkness that is light, of "luminous darkness," "sober inebriation" to quote St. Gregory of Nyssa, is to understand the movement of man in his relation to God in a transition from knowledge to love. Knowledge that leads to love mingles God's transcendence and His immanence within man's deepest part, his heart. For man to turn within and to accept the silence surrounding him as remote yet present, to accept his humility and poverty as part of his true existential being, to accept God's presence as loving and healing is to live in faith, graced by the ineffable presence of Him who grounds all human reality. It is in the silenced heart that man learns to know that God is God and learns to love Him as his Father.

3

Praying in the Heart

Have you not often had the feeling that you were really two different persons, both living inside the same body? If not two distinct persons, at least we experience from time to time that we live on different levels of consciousness. The work of such pioneers in the field of psychology and psychiatry as Sigmund Freud, Frederick W. H. Myers and Carl G. Jung has given us the terms: the conscious, the sub-conscious or unconscious, the subliminal consciousness, the collective unconscious, to describe how we can vacillate from one level of consciousness to another.

At any rate, we do feel that our "true self" has not yet been fully introduced to ourselves. We are strangers to the person that we really are! We are quite familiar to the person that others also have met. You know this person quite well. He is made up of a multitude of "characteristics" that show themselves in life's actions. He or she is the teacher, preacher, truck driver, housewife in us. That person that meets others, smiles, cries, thinks, speaks. Paul Tournier calls this our "personage." But the true person lies much deeper, below so many pre-conditionings. Deep down in you is your true self, crying out to be released, to be activated into consciousness.

Part of your true self lies in the area of the preconscious or the unconscious. Stored up in your unconscious are all the experiences that you had through your sensate life. Some of these experiences have been beautiful and possess a power to launch us into greater self-transcendence. Other experiences lie there like molten lava, ready to erupt into our conscious activities with their dark, demonic, hideous forms of non-life.

Another part is a treasure of psychical energy untapped: the area of the paranormal, psychic world. This contains the latent power of *ecstasy*, of a propulsion of ourselves out of our normal "stance" toward the Absolute that we call God. Mysticism is the actualization of the seeds in us toward union with God. This is where, according to the Fathers of the desert, the "prayer of the heart" takes place.

A CHRISTIAN TRANSCENDENTAL MEDITATION

Many today are discovering the healing power of deep, transcendental prayer, found in the prayer-disciplines of the Far Eastern religions, such as Hinduism, Zen Buddhism, and the modernized version of Transcendental Meditation (T.M.) as taught by Maharishi Mahesh Yogi. Sufism, Eastern Christian Hesychasm, and mind-control have their devotees. Such disciples discover new integration of the broken past experiences into a release of fresh, psychic energy that allows them not only to cope with their present-day problems but to function with undreamed-of creativity.

Nearly all such prayer techniques, if there results a greater expansion of consciousness in loving creativity towards others, are teaching us according to basic, common laws of our psychic structure, how to become relaxed, still-pointed, concentrated and hence to move away from an habitual beta-level of brain wave activity to the creative alpha-level.

Such techniques are *not* prayer in the Christian sense. Still they can be very helpful in preparing us for deeper prayer. What the Christian does when he is relaxed and disposed toward God determines the quality of his prayer.

The "prayer of the heart" as prayer on this deeper level of transcendence has a long tradition in Christianity, even though, for the majority of Western Christians, it is not only not known but, in some more fundamental quarters, it is even feared as a form of "occultism." (I shall deal with this problem in an appendix.) The spirituality of the Fathers of the desert, *Hesychasm*, has been still preserved in the Eastern Christian Churches, especially in the practice of the *Jesus Prayer*.[1]

THE JESUS PRAYER

From earliest times in Christianity people sought an expanded consciousness of God's abiding presence within them. They reached out for an ever-increasing awareness, constancy and sincerity in their relationship with God. The hermits that fled into the stark, barren desert were seeking an expansion of consciousness that God was truly God in their lives and they were seeking under the impulsion of the Holy Spirit that drove them into the desert, primarily of their heart, to love God with their whole heart, their whole mind, their whole strength. The heart represents this deepest part of the whole, integrated man. St. Theophan the Recluse expressed this early Christian transcendental meditation thusly:

> Prayer is turning the mind and thoughts towards God. To pray means to stand before God with the mind, mentally to gaze unswervingly at Him to converse with Him in reverent fear and hope... .The principal thing is to stand with the mind in the heart before God, and to go on standing before Him unceasingly day and night, until the end of life... .Behave as you wish, so long as you learn to stand before God with the mind in the heart, for in this lies the essence of the matter.[2]

The Desert Fathers were not running from the cities or civilization, but running into their deepest selves to find themselves on a higher level of existence. Through the prayer of the heart, they strove to live constantly in the consciousness of God's loving presence and to surrender themselves completely to His holy will.

When the Fathers urge us to such a prayer of the heart, they suggest the simple but powerful "Jesus Prayer." They had learned to enter into their deepest areas of their unconscious and there they found the demonic within themselves. They knew from faith and experience that there was no other name whereby they would be saved and healed (Acts 4:12).

The veneration of the name of Jesus is found in the very pages of the New Testament.

> But God raised Him high
> and gave Him the name
> which is above all other names
> so that all beings

in the heavens, on earth and in the underworld,
should bend the knee at the name of Jesus
and that every tongue should acclaim
Jesus Christ as Lord,
to the glory of God the Father (Phil. 2:9-11).

At first the Fathers of the desert repeated it as an oral ejaculation, much like a mantra-chant: "Lord, Jesus Christ, Son of God, have mercy on me, a sinner!" Repeated orally or with the lips, slowly and reverently, they found that it moved to the mind in silent, intellectual fixation. The highest level of conscious prayer was described as the mind moving into the heart when the prayer moved freely throughout man's deepest level of consciousness so that it became a constant, spontaneous praise-petition to God.

There was no magic in praying this prayer. There was the deep-seated faith in the risen presence of Jesus Christ as Lord and Healer and Savior. Such Christians believed that He was living within them, releasing His Holy Spirit who then prayed within them. Calling on the name of Jesus is for the Christian more than becoming aware of His existence. It is a realized, conscious experience of His abiding presence.

The name Jesus (*Ieschouah*) means Salvation of Yahweh. Jesus is the Anointed Christ, the Messiah, the royal High Priest, Lord of all creation. He is the Son of God, sharer of the Divine Life. Calling on His name and His powerful presence is to ask with confidence for His healing power of the broken parts of one's inner world of consciousness and the unconscious. It is also to release His power of transformation so that the Christian can have realized through grace the seeds of divinization locked within himself through God's creation of him according to the image and likeness that is Jesus Christ.

In teaching the Jesus Prayer, the hesychastic Fathers stress that it is a confession of faith, a self-surrender which realizes the indwelling presence of Jesus who does show mercy and heals in His condescending love. While repetition is not required, it is helpful as a mental point of internal fixation in order to ward off distractions. Here we see the common teaching of Eastern Christian prayer with that of the Far Eastern disciplines of the helpfulness of a fixation, be it a mantra (a chanted or internalized phrase easily pronounced or thought of) or an object outside of the one praying such as a crucifix, a picture, a flower, a point, a lighted candle etc. "Repetition of the prayer holds us in the remembrance of God; the remembrance of God holds us in prayer," says St. Theophan the Recluse.[3]

APPLICATIONS TO PRAYER TODAY

Can this simple form of rhythmic prayer have any value for busy Western Christians? It employs a basic technique common to all forms of "transcendental meditation." Its efficacy as true Christian prayer lies in the degree of faith, hope and love that the Holy Spirit constantly infuses into our hearts to "know Jesus Christ and to experience the power of His resurrection and to suffer with Him" (Phil. 3:10).

By breathing rhythmically while letting the senses and imagination concentrate on the words of the prayer, the Christian reaches a depth of tranquillity wherein his higher self is freed of lesser pre-conditionings to pray on a more nearly total level of self-surrender to the living presence of Jesus Lord.

In all true prayerful experiences, the Christian enters into the awesome presence of God as holy. His transcendent beauty and power overwhelm us. How simply the Jesus Prayer puts it: "Lord, Jesus Christ, Son of God." Jesus is Lord of the universe, Creator, Alpha and Omega. In Him all things are created. All things reach fulfillment through Him. Yet He is also Jesus, Healer. "I have come that you might have life, life more abundantly" (Jn. 10:10). He is *Christos*, the anointed Messiah, the long-awaited Son of God. "God so loved the world as to give us His only begotten Son so that anyone who believes in Him shall not perish, but have eternal life" (Jn. 3:16). Man in prayer is convicted by the Holy Spirit to see in contrast to the mountain of Jesus' holiness the valley of his own sinfulness. And so he cries out from the darkness of the bondage that holds him captive, that Jesus have mercy, the *hesed* Covenant of healing given to God's *Anawim* that confess their need of healing. "Lord, that I may see."

The poverty felt in the desert of our hearts fills us with a searing thirst for the Living Water. Like pilgrims we cry out hungrily for the Bread of Life. We stretch out to possess the Unpossessable, to encompass Him who is without limits. The Beatitude is a realized experience: "Blessed are those who hunger and thirst for justice, for they shall be filled."

Hence the use of the Jesus Prayer will vary, depending on the degree of advancement in prayer life and interior faith. It can be a simple ejaculation used as we go about our daily work, synchronized with our breathing and thus allowing us to remain conscious of Jesus' presence within us.

REACHING THE STILL POINT

In our fixed periods of prayer the Jesus Prayer can serve as a means of centering ourselves upon the indwelling Trinity, of allowing us to reach that inner "still point." For more advanced contemplatives, it will lead them into the presence of the Lord beyond all words and forms about God, when even the words of the Jesus Prayer will cease in utter silence and the prayer of heart-to-heart takes over, the *ignita oratio* (the fiery prayer) of Cassian.

Through fidelity to this simple prayer that integrates the body, soul and spirit into a prayerful whole person, the Christian begins to enter into the priestly prayer of Jesus Christ and His priestly transfiguring action going on in the world.

The Christian breathes and with his breath he is conscious of breathing forth the transfiguring power of Jesus as Lord of the cosmos. Jesus Christ leads the Christian into a lived experience of the Holy Spirit who in turn reveals to the Christian the meaning of the presence of Jesus as Lord and Healer and also of the Father as *Abba*.

In that living experience of the indwelling Trinity, the Christian begins to experience at each moment the Father begetting His children in Christ Jesus through His Spirit of love. The Christified man of the Jesus Prayer moves out into his busy world filled with love of God and with God's love for His world. He offers himself as a reconciler of the whole world according to St. Paul's vision of the Cosmic Christ.

A LIFE IN CHRIST JESUS

The Jesus Prayer is, therefore, more than a prayer to be said. It is ultimately a life in Christ Jesus. Grace is no longer a *thing* we pray for, but it is the uncreated Energies of God's presence made known to our consciousness as we humbly cry out in our darkness for the healing power of Jesus Lord. The name of Jesus called out unceasingly leads us into His holy presence. He sends the Spirit into our hearts to reveal the infinite love of the Father for His children.

This is the prayer of the heart; it is the way to the incessant prayer of the early Fathers. It still has great meaning for us all. "Jesus Christ the same yesterday, today and always." Lord, Jesus Christ, Son of God, have mercy on me a sinner.

From my description of the Jesus Prayer, a reader should not feel any pressure, thinking that one can experience a deeper, transcendental, Christian prayer only by using this particular method or form of prayer. This is of course not true. Even using the formula: "Lord, Jesus Christ, Son of God, have mercy on me a sinner," one can change the formulation in any way that is easy to repeat consistently and meaningfully. The important element is the name of *Jesus*. This invocation has always been held in the highest regard and believed to be extremely powerful in all ages of Christianity. St. Gregory of Sinai writes:

> The gift which we received from Jesus Christ in holy baptism is not destroyed but only buried as a treasure in the ground. And both common sense and gratitude demand that we should take care to unearth this treasure and bring it to light. This can be done in two ways. The gift of baptism is revealed first of all

by painstaking fulfillment of the commandments; the more we carry these out, the more clearly the light shines upon us in its true splendor and brilliance. Secondly, it comes to light and is revealed through the continual invocation of the Lord Jesus, or by unceasing remembrance of God, which is one and the same thing. The first method is powerful but the second is more so; so much so that even fidelity to the commandments receives its full strength from prayer. For this reason, if we truly desire to bring to flower the seed of grace that is hidden within us, we should hasten to acquire the habit of this exercise of the heart, and always practice this prayer within it, without any image or form, until it warms our mind and inflames our soul with an inexpressible love towards God and men.[4]

In 1925 *The Way of a Pilgrim* was revealed to the West.[5] The work tells of a man's search for an experience of God and a way to salvation. He finds a book called the *Philokalia* which becomes his instructor in the mystical experience. With practice he develops the "prayer of the heart" which, as we have said, is the ultimate in the prayer experience. Aside from the invocation of the name of Jesus, breathing control becomes a natural and essential part of the method. In the structure of the prayer itself an inhaling and exhaling, conceptually as well as physically, is intrinsic. "Lord Jesus Christ, Son of God," is the reaching upward into the transcendent which corresponds to the exhaling. Its counterpart, "have mercy upon me," is the drawing of the transcendent into the immanent self, obviously through inhaling.

This prayer is begun vocally in a soft whisper which then drops to a sub-vocal movement of the lips. At this point, the focus is on the meaning accompanied by the physical rhythm. With practice the phrase becomes more natural, eventually dropping to complete silence. With this silence and concentration the rest of the body becomes still and relaxed. The heart slows, the breath drops to a minimum, the neck may bend slightly and the body experiences a rest deeper than sleep. If this method is not done properly, serious complications may ensue, for instance, nausea or even fainting. It is for this reason that Eastern Christian writers normally insist that anyone practising the method should be under close guidance of an experienced spiritual director.[6]

The method is very similar to other Eastern practices. In my own experience I find it almost identical to transcendental meditation which, instead of the Jesus phrase, uses a Sanscrit mantra. There are times when it is unhealthy to use this technique of meditation, for instance, on a full stomach or while under the influence of drugs. However, when used properly the effects of the Jesus Prayer and transcendental meditation edify the existential experience of everyday life and deepen the sensitivity of the person to his environment and self.

One must carefully consider the motivation which stimulates the desire to meditate. The motivation must always be a desire to experience and deepen the inner life, not to escape the outer one. The latter is illustrated in *Franny and Zooey* by J. D. Salinger. Franny, a college girl, finding both her egotistical and materialistic boyfriend and society repulsive, takes refuge in the Jesus Prayer which she has discovered in reading *The Way of a Pilgrim.* She eventually faints from fasting yet pursues an introverted lifestyle which upsets her family. She continues "praying ceaselessly" until through her brother Zooey she realizes that escaping is no escape at all. Until she understands what is happening outside of her, that is, school, friends, teachers, family, etc., she cannot begin to know her interior self. When Zooey, coerced by his mother, goes into her room to talk to her, he says:

> I'm not bringing this up with the idea of throwing anything back in your teeth — my God. I'm bringing this up for a good reason. I'm bringing it up because I don't think you understood Jesus when you were a child and I don't think you understand him now. I think you've got him confused in your mind with about five or ten other religious personages, and I don't see how you can go ahead with the Jesus Prayer until you know who's who and what's what.[7]

Escape from life for a period of time can re-create man so that he is better able to cope with his moral existence. However, methods of escape such as alcohol or drugs only leave him where he left off. In the case of Franny, the Jesus Prayer was abused by substituting it for a pain-killer. With the rapid pace of the twentieth century and the noise of modern technology, attention to the interior self is of paramount importance. However, to cut off people as well as the physical environment remains a constant danger. The interior life is a place for recreation and integration, where the whole man encounters the whole universe as well as its Creator. To use the Jesus Prayer for anything less than this is not only a mistake and an abuse, but a grave danger as well.

One does not seek to pray in a Christian, transcendental manner merely to relax or to be able to cope with one's problems. He seeks not mere vacuity of mind which has nothing to do with Christian prayer but can easily prevent one from approaching God in deep faith. To relax and reach a state of creative "being" is not prayer. What we do when we have reached this stage of "integration" spells how deeply we will be praying.

I would like to outline here a method in the hope that Christians may find this helpful in praying deeper and receiving more complete healing of one's entire being on the physical, psychical and spiritual levels. Again, I reiterate, one must not become attached to words or mere techniques but one must push himself in deep faith inwardly to find the indwelling Trinity and there in adoration and submission yield oneself completely to the Absolute God. One will adjust any technique therefore to fit into that faith framework and not vice versa.

PHYSICAL RELAXATION

Too often Westerners "jump" into prayer as though they were attacking some conquerable force. They too readily forget the body and where they personally "are at" in reference to the world around them. The body is a tremendous field of chemical and electrical charges, interacting with the world around it. It is imperative that man begin to pray by starting to relax the body and bring it into the "heart," into man's deepest concentration in stillness or into as total an integration of body, soul and spirit as is possible.

We can pray on a subway but the deepest type of prayer necessitates transcending our habitual activities to move into a psychological state of deep silence, of waiting on the Lord. For this, choose a quiet place; sit in a very relaxed position. Many find sitting on a cushion in the lotus position helpful. If one sits on a chair, it should be a straight chair that allows one to keep the spinal cord straight up and down with no humping of the shoulders.

We are now ready to put ourselves into a prayerful attitude of body and mind. Breathe deeply filling the abdominal cavity with air. Much of our tension can be removed if we breathe diaphragmatically. As you breathe in, feel the diaphragm muscle in the abdominal area extend itself outwardly. As you slowly breathe outwardly you find the diaphragm seemingly moving inwardly. Feel that basic rhythm, so much like the ebb and flow of the ocean tide.

Close your eyes and try to concentrate on your body, on all the parts individually, relaxing all the time each part as you concentrate on it. Start with the top of the head, the forehead, the eyelids. Relax the tenseness in the nerves of your eyes, your cheeks, chin. Let your up-tight shoulders relax without sagging them. Concentrate on your chest, your heart area, your abdomen, the genital area. Relax your arms, elbows, wrists, hands, fingers. Let go of the tenseness in your hips, your thighs, knees, calves, ankles and toes. Let go of tension, believing by faith that God is present in all parts of your body that is a temple of God. Breathe deeply and enjoy that presence of God within you. Stretch out spiritually in adoration, trust, in loving surrender. Let go of the control of your life and experience the pulsating energies of the love of God within you. Desire to love God in return.

COUNT DOWN

Picture in your mind that you are on the 20th floor of a building and you enter an elevator that will take you very slowly down to the basement. As you count each number, feel yourself passing deeper and deeper into your inner self, into your "heart." Stop at each number, each floor of your consciousness, and tell yourself that you are becoming more relaxed: "19....I am relaxed all over....18...go down deeper into my inner self....17....it feels so wonderful to be free....16....I am letting go of my life....15...14...13...12....I feel like a bird floating effortlessly in the sky; no resistance....11...10....God is coming to meet me....9...8...I feel almost weightless as I have felt sometimes floating in water...7...I am going deeper and deeper into myself...6.there I will meet God and all will be peace and joyful, fresh and full of new life...5....Come Lord, Jesus....4...like a candle in the middle of a long cave, no flickering, no movement, just the still point...3...God, how good it is to be here....2...I am being refreshed by cool, running waters...1...getting closer to Him, my Strength...0...I am totally relaxed and at peace."

Breathe in and out rhythmically and begin to think mentally your Christian mantra: "Lord, Jesus Christ," as you breathe in. "Son of God," as you breathe out. "Have mercy on me," as you breathe in. "A sinner," as you breathe out. Repeat again, lengthening your breathing, while you maintain the state of relaxation. When you feel yourself in the presence of God, the Almighty, the Holy of Holies, let go of the words. They can serve as a point of fixation if you find after a few minutes of "floating" in the presence of God's sea of love that you are becoming diffused and distracted.

If the Christian mantra of the Jesus Prayer seems too long, you might want to reduce it simply to the words: "Jesus"...."mercy;"or "Jesus"...."I love You." The true

Christian prayer begins when we become deeply aware of the presence of Jesus. He releases His Spirit of love and we are enabled to pray in the Spirit. The Jesus Prayer becomes similar to praying in tongues. One is not concerned with the words or thoughts that the words or sounds might conjure up. It is rather a point of fixation that allows us to move from a rational communication with God to a meta-rational listening to God speak His Word to us through His Holy Spirit. This is what St. Paul referred to when he told us that our controlled prayer is not the highest but, when we yield to the Spirit of Jesus Christ, we pray in our heart and touch the very heart of God Himself.

> The Spirit too comes to help us in our weakness. For when we cannot choose words in order to pray properly, the Spirit Himself expresses our plea in a way that could never be put into words, and God who knows everything in our hearts knows perfectly well what he means, and that the pleas of the saints expressed by the Spirit are according to the mind of God (Rom. 8:26-27).

4

Prayer as Healing

God is the fullness of life. Man was created to share continually in God's life. This means that man would expand in his conscious awareness of God's love making it possible for man to share in His life. But instead we see man locked inside himself, sick, anemic, afraid, cut off from inter-communion with God and fellow-man.

We sense a keen frustration within us because there sounds a deep echo through the labyrinthian alleys and deadends of our memory that we were made for a greater share in life. We were meant to be "whole" people. Instead, we feel our disintegration. Our body wars against the soul, the soul slashes out at our inner spirit.

Man invents games and roles he can play to give himself the impression he is happy and healthy. He pursues like a lonely hunter his prey, thinking money, fame, power, sexual fulfillment will bring him the life he so desperately wants. Yet he always falls back defeated by himself. The enemy is within himself! He is his own Oedipean killer.

And one day there sounds within him a call to be more than he is. "I want to be whole! I want freedom from myself!" he cries. Thus he begins his journey toward the Fountain of Life.

St. Macarius of Egypt saw man's healing integration as tied with penitence and purification:

> Unless a man turns toward God of his own free will and with all his longing, unless he cries to Him in prayer with complete faith, he cannot be cured.[1]

All of us feel the disorientation within our members. The body is a drag, bringing us pain, exhaustion, a heaviness that was not meant to be when God created us. Our minds bind us also with their distracting thoughts, even demonic suggestions, their tenuous grasp on a very limited area of knowledge that so easily can pass into forgetfulness or error through age and emotional stresses. Man's greatest frustration is to feel he was made for greater fulfillment and yet he sees his "low performance." St. Paul captures this confining imprisonment within himself and the need to break out into freedom by the power of Jesus Christ.

> ...but I am unspiritual; I have been sold as a slave to sin. I cannot understand my own behavior. I fail to carry out the things I want to do, and I find myself doing the very things I hate....The fact is, I know of nothing good living in me — living, that is, in my unspiritual self — for though the will to do what is good is in me, the performance is not, with the result that instead of doing the good things I want to do, I carry out the sinful things I do not want. When I act against my will, then, it is not my true self doing it, but sin which lives in me....In my inmost self I dearly love God's Law, but I can see that my body follows a different law that battles against the law which my reason dictates. This is what makes me a prisoner of that law of sin which lives inside my body. What a wretched man I am! Who will rescue me from this body

doomed to death? Thanks be to God through Jesus Christ our Lord! (Rom. 7:14-24).

JESUS CHRIST—LOVE INCARNATE

After years of pondering my own existential situation and seeing it mirrored in the lives of the people to whom I have tried to bring Christ during my years of priestly ministry, I am more and more convinced that the one great sin in all of our lives is to live in the darkness and ignorance that prevent us from knowing by an experience that God truly loves us. This one root-sin, man's loneliness, is from what he seeks by plays of power to extricate himself. The things we do called sins are nothing but manifestations of our desire to show ourselves and others that we are worthy of being loved. Our terrifying isolation and locked-in condition force us to do all sorts of "sinful" actions, but the basic sin is one of ignorance: we simply have not experienced the truth that God loves us greatly and hence we have no reason for being lonely.

But even though God has spoken to us through His prophets of old and assured us that He does love us, we would not believe. It was just too incredible that God should love us! But the Good News is that God really does love us and to prove this He sent us His incarnated Image, Jesus Christ. "Yes, God loved the world so much that He gave His only Son, so that everyone who believes in Him may not be lost but may have eternal life" (Jn. 3:16).

The condescending mercy of God adapts itself to man's condition and becomes enfleshed so that in human language, especially the language of love that speaks the loudest and clearest, suffering unto death, God's love would be spoken for each person who would care to hear this Word of love. God's plan to heal man's loneliness is to give him His only Begotten Son, Jesus Christ, to act out in terms of human suffering, the infinite love of the Father.

Jesus Christ is the perfect image of the invisible God (Col. 1:15). We have no other way of knowing the Father but through His Word made flesh. Jesus not only preaches to us about the great love of this Father, but He acts out this love. Throughout His whole public life Jesus went about doing good, especially in the form of healing all types of sicknesses and diseases. He is never more the perfect image of the Heavenly Father than when He saw the multitudes fainting and being scattered abroad as sheep without a shepherd and He was moved with compassion (Matt. 9:36).

If human fathers know how to give good gifts, how much more the Heavenly Father wants to give us the very best gift. Jesus insists over and over in His preaching that if we ask anything of the Father in His name, the Father will grant it. It gives great glory to the Father that we pray in the name of Jesus. Man needs no longer to be afraid or lonely. His Heavenly Father knows all of his needs and He will provide for them if only man will become like a little child and surrender his whole life to that Father.

But Jesus Christ, the Image of the Father, would not be content merely to tell us all these wonderful things about the Heavenly Father. If He didn't go further, even to the point of the awful *kenosis*, the emptying of Himself in total giving on the Cross for us, we could always have asked God to do more. If God didn't go all the way to act out His infinite, perfect love for us, would we not wonder whether St. John's definition of God as Love would need proving?

But God the Father did go all the way by giving us the perfect mirror, Jesus Christ, in whom we could see once and for all that God is truly Love. As He himself said, whoever sees Him, sees the Father (Jn. 14:9). This *kenotic* love that Jesus manifests so poignantly on the Cross is unto His glory.

> His state was divine
> yet He did not cling
> to His equality with God
> but emptied Himself
> to assume the condition of a slave
> and became as men are;
> and being as all men are,
> He was humbler yet,
> even to accepting death,
> death on a cross.
> But God raised Him high
> and gave Him the name
> which is above all other names
> so that all beings
> in the heavens, on earth and
> in the underworld,
> should bend the knee at the name of Jesus
> and that every tongue should acclaim
> Jesus Christ as Lord,
> to the glory of God the Father (Phil. 2:6:11).

JESUS HEALS

Jesus Christ redeems us by healing us. St. Antony of the desert (d. 350) describes Christ as the "Great Physician:" "...God, seeing that the wound grows wide and demands drastic treatment, determined to send down His only-begotten Son, who is our only Physician."[2] But He heals through His Holy Spirit who abounds in our hearts (Rom. 5:5). This Spirit is the Love of the Father and the Son. He makes it possible through His infused gifts of faith, hope and love that we can experience the love of God for us made manifest in Christ Jesus.

> God's love for us was revealed
> when God sent into the world
> His only Son so that we could
> have life through Him. . :
> when He sent His Son to be the
> sacrifice that takes our sins away (1 Jn. 4:9-10).

The blood of Christ redeems us through the power of the Holy Spirit who reveals to us the depths of God's love for us individually. ". . .to win salvation through our Lord Jesus Christ, who died for us so that, alive or dead, we should still live united to Him" (1 Thess. 5:10).

Only the Holy Spirit can give us this experiential knowledge as a gift when we are poor in spirit and receptive to this infusion. "The Spirit reaches the depths of everything, even the depths of God. . . .we have received the Spirit that comes from God, to teach us to understand the gifts that He has given us" (1 Cor. 2:10-12).

What the Holy Spirit teaches us is an abiding experience that God loves us infinitely in His love made manifest through Jesus' dying for us.

> The life I now live in this body,
> I live in faith: faith in the Son
> of God who loved me and who sacrificed
> Himself for my sake (Gal. 2:20).

St. Paul was so convinced that the death of Jesus was to be experienced as an outpouring of God's love so as to change our lives. "...and the reason He died for all was so that living men should live no longer for themselves, but for Him who died and was raised to life for them" (2 Cor. 5:15).

"For me He dies" is St. Paul's constant experience through the Holy Spirit. This is what he desires more of — this intimate, experiential knowledge of Jesus Christ. He counts everything as rubbish if only he can have Jesus Christ and be given a place in Him (Phil. 3:8-9).

> All I want is to know Christ and
> the power of His resurrection and
> to share His sufferings by reproducing
> the pattern of His death....
> I am still running, trying to capture
> the prize for which Christ Jesus
> capture me (Phil. 3:10-12).

It is the unique role of the Holy Spirit through His revelation to us about God's great love in Christians and Jesus that heals us. St. Gregory of Nyssa teaches that the Spirit of love is a healing fire that transforms the Christians, "when such, then, have been purged from evil and utterly removed by the healing processes worked out by fire...."[3]

FAITH IN JESUS WHO HEALS

When Jesus showed compassion on the broken people brought to Him for healing, He was imaging the condescending mercy of His Father. Yet over and over again He healed the crowds of sick persons only when they were able to *believe* in Him. Wanting to be healed and believing that Jesus could heal them, they were opening themselves to a deeper faith of the Holy Spirit to accept Jesus and His healing message of love. He praised the blind Bartimaeus on the road to Jericho "Go; your faith has saved (healed) you" (Mk. 10:52). Also a leper was healed because of his faith in Jesus (Lk. 17:19). Jesus told the woman suffering from a hemorrhage, "My daughter, your faith has restored you to health; go in peace and be free from your complaint" (Mk. 5:34).

Jesus is not merely concerned with spiritual healing — forgiving sinners their sins. He, like a loving father, is touched with pity and heals *all* manner of sickness, affecting the body, soul or spirit. He is desirous of giving more abundant life to all levels of man's living.

Yet in His own public life Jesus did not heal persons who did not receive Him with faith. We read that in Nazareth He could heal only a few persons because of His fellow-townsmen's lack of faith in Him (Mk. 5:25).

A PRAYERFUL ENCOUNTER

For believing Christians, Jesus Christ can still be encountered. He lives deep down, within the "heart" of man. He promised that He and the Father would come and abide within the Christian (Jn. 14:23). At the center of our being, we can still fall down and confess our belief that Jesus Christ is the Son of God. We can cry out to Him that we are broken in body, soul and spirit.

He releases His Spirit who reveals that Jesus Christ is always of the same mind-set as that which He had on

Calvary. "For me He dies!" becomes an experience that leads me into the awesome presence of the Heavenly Father as perfect holiness, beauty and love. I become at last centered in my heart as I experience the "pulling" together of my frightened spirit, my weary body, my scattered mind.

I learn to yield to His healing love. I allow myself to be loved! I enter into a new freedom of a child of God, loved so deeply by God Himself. I surrender to His love and peace pours over me like a soft rain falling gently on dry ground. My potential for *being* expands into a realized consciousness. I am being healed! The Lord is my good Shepherd. Whom shall I fear?

> In meadows of green grass He lets me lie.
> To the waters of repose He leads me;
> there He revives my soul.
>
> He guides me by paths of virtue
> for the sake of His name.
>
> Though I pass through a gloomy valley,
> I fear no harm;
> beside me your rod and your staff
> are there, to hearten me.
>
> Ah, how goodness and kindness pursue me,
> every day of my life:
> my home, the house of Yahweh,
> as long as I live! (Ps. 23:2-4,6).

I feel in the depths of my being a new transformation taking place. Powers to love, to-be-towards God, towards myself in a healthy way, towards others open up slowly like the locked-in petals of a bedewed rose gently let go and expose a new harmony of many things captured in the union of one flower of exquisite beauty.

The chaotic past, those dried bones of yester-year, receive the soft breath of God's Spirit of Love and they become enfleshed into my newly transformed being. The past friends and enemies, persons and events treated so indifferently by me, all take on new meaning. Like Lazarus, I have heard the Divine Physician cry out, "Lazarus, here! Come out!" (Jn. 11:43).

I come out of the past. ". . .feet and hands bound with bands of stuff and a cloth round his face. Jesus said, 'Unbind him, let him go free' " (Jn. 11:44). As I sit in deep, silent prayer, repeating the healing name of 'Lord, Jesus Christ, Son of God, have mercy on me a sinner,' I experience a healing freedom.

An expanded consciousness floods my whole being as I feel the body, soul, spirit relationships within me come together in an integrated, whole person. "God, it is good to be alive and healthy!" I realize the Divine uncreated Energies of God's Triadic life flowing through me, in every part, on every level. I am a branch and God is the vine. I breathe in His breath. I am alive with His life. Like a butterfly, with wet, tightly-packed wings, I stretch upward towards the Heavenly Kingdom. The wings dry, strengthen, life me aloft to new, dizzying heights of union with God.

I pour out my life in complete adoration of my God and Savior. *Ecstasy* is truly a standing outside and beyond my habitual self, a transcending impulsion toward God. There is "inner identity." I now know through experience the *why* of my existence. I have been made by God to share in His Being, He is Love and in being loved by Him and my loving Him in return I *am* what I was made to be. I am healed and now raised to a new existence in Jesus Christ. The resurrection is a healing that takes place even now before death as I experience God as Love in prayer.

Through the healing power of Christ's Spirit of Love experienced in prayer and in the sacramental encounter with Christ as Healer in Penance and the Holy Eucharist, the Christian knows a new-founded peace and joy which pervade his whole life (Gal. 5:22; Phil. 4:4).

HEALING OTHERS

God in His infinite mercy heals us in deep prayer. As we have been healed of our loneliness and isolation by experiencing His love for us in Christ Jesus, to that degree we can be healing love to those around us. We are called to mediate God's love within us to others by our touches, our looks of sympathy and loving understanding, by our words uttered in humble reverence for the uniqueness of our neighbor, by our acts of kind service done to the least of God's creatures.

I have a banner hanging in my room that I look at each day with the words:

In loving one another,
God in us is made flesh.

God in His humility has tied His healing power of love to the love of Him experienced in us in prayer that urges us to incarnate the same Word-enfleshed Love of Jesus Christ in the lives of others.

I give you a new commandment:
love one another;
just as I have loved you,
you also must love one another.
By this love you have for one another,
everyone will know that you are my
disciples (Jn. 13:34-35).

The Christian knows that through his Baptism He is pledged to "putting on Jesus Christ." He shares in Jesus Christ's eternal priesthood of bringing all things back to the Father. "And all things are of God who has reconciled us to Himself by Jesus Christ and has given to us the ministry of reconciliation" (2 Cor. 5:18).

Jesus Christ extends His healing love to others through our concrete love toward them. How humbling a thought it is that Jesus heals or does not heal others by the love of God that we allow or fail to radiate out to others.

Recently this truth came home to me powerfully in the following example. A woman, 32 years old, twice divorced, was on the verge of insanity. Doctors said they could do nothing for her unless she agreed to enter the state hospital for the mentally sick. When she came to me, it was evident that this woman was very close to total despair. Her constant complaint was: "No one cares for me. No one has time to listen to me." I heard her story, a classical case of rejection by her parents at an early age. She continually heard from those who should have loved her that she was no good, a complete failure at everything she did.

In a beautiful sharing several of us Christians were able to pray with her; but more importantly we were able to show her genuine love. She was excited like a little child discovering a great, new treasure. She had a beautiful singing voice and we told her so. She was wanted. She found a new dignity. I could hardly believe what I saw two months later when I again met her. This Christian community had given her love and a sense of dignity. She blossomed beautifully into a person of happiness and calm.

Every time we meet a person we are preparing ourselves for a healing, prayerful encounter to the degree that we open ourselves to the Christ in that person; to the degree of Christ-life that that person lets flow into our being by his love toward us.

Prayer of the heart is a state of health that we first experience within us in deep prayer. According to the love of God received by us in prayer, we are enabled by God's loving presence to open up to each person that we meet and let God's healing love pour into that person. Prayer that at its heart is a deep experience of the love of Jesus Christ for me personally will also be a transforming and healing love towards others.

We love others with the love of God Himself. And as we touch others and let the healing power of God pour into their lives, so also we receive, in giving love, an increase in healing love. A process goes on infinitely of being healed by God's love in prayer in order to love others and heal them of their loneliness, only to be healed more completely of our own isolation as we love them, only to be healthier now to love others more.

This is another way of describing prayer: receiving the personalized love of God for us, made manifest in Christ Jesus, and in the healing love, to continue prayerfully to find and serve God in others. Prayer is healing

because prayer is to experience God's love that gives us
new life. Having a new life, we share it with others and
thus they too receive more of health, more of God's life.

> . . .as long as we love one another
> God will live in us
> and His love will be complete in us.
> . . .God is love
> and anyone who lives in love lives in God,
> and God lives in Him.
> . . .We are to love, then,
> because He loved us first. (1 Jn. 4:12,16,19).

5

Jesus Christ — Lord of My Unconscious

Nietzsche wrote in *Thus Spake Zarathustra*: "I could believe only in a God that would know how to dance." This phrase suggests to me a God who knows joy. He is excited with life and He dances to communicate His inner dynamism outwardly. It recalls the parable of the Prodigal Son and the dancing and merriment because the father has refound his lost son. It suggests the exuberant imaging used by Jesus Christ of the eternal Feast, the Banquet, that is Food of fire and light, giving eternal life and love to all who sit at the Father's table.

It also calls to my mind T. S. Eliot's powerful description of God's eternal life as our source of true life — a dance at the still point.

> At the still point of the turning world. Neither flesh
> nor fleshless;
> Neither from nor towards; at the still point,
> there the dance is,
> But neither arrest nor movement. And do not call it fixity.
> Where past and future are gathered. Neither movement
> from nor towards,

Neither ascent nor decline. Except for the point,
   the still point,
There would be no dance, and there is only the dance.
I can only say, there we have been; but I cannot say where.
And I cannot say, how long, for that is to place it in time.

(Burt Norton)

To enter into God's dance of exuberant joy and
fullness of life, we must descend. This descent is a descent
into the deepest reaches of our consciousness and our
unconscious. It is really an ascent to God who dwells in
the secret recesses of our hearts. It is simply growing into
greater, expanded consciousness through *prayer*. And yet
how few people dare to move toward that dance!

We used to peg the people we didn't like as
conservatives if we were liberal, liberals if we were
conservative. Another convenient grouping of people was
the younger and older generations. Today I feel the *real*
difference that separates humans is the difference between
persons (young and old) who live predominantly on a
sensory level and others who live on a level of greater
expanded consciousness.

This first group is the object at which the typical
American advertisement on T.V. is aimed. Such value
above all else, body comfort, no pain, to eat and sleep
well, body beauty and physical health. The second group
embraces the smaller segment of humanity that is pushing
always to greater synthesis of knowledge, a greater
experience of the unified meaning of life with man's
directing all his energies towards that ultimacy.

TOWARD EXPANDED CONSCIOUSNESS

For me it has been an interesting experience, while

teaching for the past 13 years at Fordham University, to observe almost a steady movement (sometimes a bit staggering with weaving in and out!!) in an evolution towards what it means to be a human being. In the early 60's there was among the students, those forerunners of where the action is, the great social and political involvement as the students strove to bring about racial equality, peace through anti-war demonstrations and the right-to-life protests by lying down in the roads to be run over. Then they tripped on acid or found the Dionysian hills of open sexual freedom. Deep behind all of this we find a frenetic thirst for expanded consciousness, a defiant rebellion against being a statistic or a digit, a dehumanized cog.

Their music, styles of hair, clothing, dancing, singing, theater, painting and sculpture of this decade show a violent rebellion against the static "clear and distinct" Cartesian forms. There must be more to life than what the suburbia of their bourgeois parents were so busily striving to possess. On stage this Dionysian frenzy of bodily sensation ran the gamut from topless to bottomless to nude. The Living Theater and Open Theater saw actors running all over, advocating wild freedom and animal license as a reaction to an outdated Puritan type of morality. The world, that had based its dreams of happiness on science and reason, put it all into neat boxes and labeled them, but it had forgotten the most important element, human love. So flower-power became the cry!

They were reading in class that life was absurd because there was the inexplicable mysterious quality of our lives that Strinberg, Jarry, Pirandello, Ionesco, Beckett and Genet were writing about. The students were frantically asking: is there any other alternative to human existence? Is there any alternative to the either/or of rationalism vs. irrationalism?

In the late 60's the students found the Jesus Movement in some quarters. They discovered the Bible and Jesus who was loving them. He became their hero, worship, rebel for peace, their Superstar. Johnny Cash, Pat Boone, Judy Collins, Eric Clapton were singing and playing about "My Sweet Lord" and His "Amazing Grace."

The 70's rolled in with a powerful *Drang am Osten.* The Far-Eastern religions, Hindu, Yoga, Zen Buddhism, the Tibetan Book of the Dead, Gurdieff, occultism, Edgar Cacey were common bits of conversation after the music died down. The students were into meditation and blowing the mind by Transcendental Meditation, Silva Mind Control, Hypnosis, Arica, process meditation, transactional analysis. But it wasn't just the students but older men and women turned to meditation to feel the healing of body, soul and spirit. They found that such discipline not only removed anxieties but opened up areas of the unconscious that they never suspected existed, except in their "wildest dreams." Creative powers were being unleashed. ESP powers of clairvoyance, telepathy, psychokinesis, Theta experiences out of the body, communing with the dead became favorite reading for all ages.

The 70's will be noted by this unique interest in and experimenting on the part of the ordinary "lay-person" with expansion of consciousness. No doubt the rise in anxieties and stresses in daily living, the inability to cope with the speed of urban life and the meaninglessness of it all pushed most "seekers" into the area of transcendent, psychic experiences as a way to avoid mental illness and to survive from day to day.

PERSONALISM IN RELIGION

We can also see this same movement towards greater consciousness invading the arena of religion. A built-in danger in all religions is the tendency on the part of man to settle for the trappings, the extrinsic forms of worship and dogma instead of continuing to grow through an intensive asceticism of purification of one's interior and a silent listening in one's heart to the wild God of the desert speak to him. Man is always repeating the game of the Israelites in the desert who became tired of adoring a God they could not see, so they built themselves a golden calf that they could easily materialize. Then they knew just where they were in regard to the god they constructed. They were easily in power and religion became another move towards self-power and pride.

It was Carl G. Jung who pointed out to the impoverished West that it had lost the ability to meet God through myths, symbols and archetypal models implanted in man's unconscious whereby he can commune with the Transcendent Absolute in a world closed to the senses and intellect of man. Western man, in all of his aggressive assault against nature to dominate it and control it, to transform it according to man's whims or his idea of what a good, "human" world should be like, lost the ability to listen in silent contemplation to that inner Voice.

More positively, many Christians, before a world torn by violence and great oppressive injustices, by hunger and crime, are beginning to ask themselves just what does it mean to be a Christian. I, after so many years of "brain-washing" and habituation through cultic practices, can easily relate to God when I want. I can praise God and thank Him. I can even forgive my worst enemies, at least in word, as I stand before the altar of the Lord. But how deep does my Christianity go?

When a building constructor plans to build on a certain site, he usually seeks to know the consistency of the soil that will be under his building. A drill goes down and up comes the various layers of soil. I have often thought: if they ever could invent a similar machine that could enter into my mind, I wonder how far down I would find Jesus Christ?

I am very much aware that I can live a very superficial life as a Christian. It even becomes convenient. I can be a Christian when *I* want to! At other times I possess the ability to block out that area that says: you are a Christian, you should want to act in this way; please don't stifle the Spirit by doing that! And in those moments when I turn away, when I allow the deeper areas of my being to take over and control my consciousness, I find that I am an average pagan, a man of this world, the flesh and the devil. I ask myself as often as I can because I don't trust a great portion of my life that seems to be beyond my habitual control: How much of my life is under the actual dominance of Jesus Christ? How much of my life is beyond my immediate control?

St. Paul meditated many years in the silent Arabian Desert and discovered deep down within him an inner enemy that was seeking to destroy the God-life within him.

> ...but I am unspiritual; I have been sold as a slave to sin. I cannot understand my own behavior. I fail to carry out the things I want to do, and I find myself doing the very things I hate...In fact, this seems to be the rule, that every single time I want to do good it is something evil that comes to hand. In

my inmost self I dearly love God's Law, but I can see that my
body follows a different law that battles against the law which
my reason dictates. This is what makes me a prisoner of that
law of sin which lives inside my body. What a wretched man I
am! Who will rescue me from this body doomed to death?
Thanks be to God through Jesus Christ our Lord! (Rom.
7:14-24).

We all can understand the Doctor Jekyll and Mr.
Hyde within St. Paul because we possess the same inner
principle that wars to destroy the Christi-life in us. We can
control the surface sometimes. Society with its "proper"
way that we should act in certain circumstances, not doing
some things just because it is not the agreed custom does
help us in this external control. But beneath this "proper-
ness" all too often, at least, I find a seething volcano of
self-love, hatred towards certain individuals, readiness to
use violence to get my own way. The jungle is very much
within me underneath the external polish of an educated
person. "The Lord of the Flies" is experienced by all of us
if we have any self-knowledge at all.

St. Paul exhorts us: "Do not model yourselves on the
behavior of the world around you, but let your behavior
change, modelled by your new mind. This is the only way
to discover the will of God and know what is good, what it
is that God wants, what is the perfect thing to do" (Rom.
12:2).

We are to be transformed in our minds and this would
include my whole mind, intellect, will, imagination,
consciousness and unconscious. All of me must be brought
under the healing power of Jesus Christ. Again St. Paul
exhorts us to enter into this interior battle and take every
thought captive to be put under the loving submission to

Jesus Christ: "Every thought is our prisoner, captured to be brought into obedience to Christ. Once you have given your complete obedience, we are prepared to punish any disobedience" (2 Cor. 10:5-6).

Yes, I want to belong entirely to Jesus Christ so that I put on His mind completely and I live no longer myself but He lives in me (Gal. 2:20). It would be great to follow through St. Paul's exhortation: "Your mind must be renewed by a spiritual revolution so that you can put on the new self that has been created in God's way, in the goodness and holiness of the truth" (Ephes. 4:23-24).

If God has created me according to Jesus Christ, the perfect Image of the Heavenly Father (Col. 1:15), then it should be possible for me to attain unto this fullness to which I have been predestined by His grace. I am a part of them that ". . .are the ones He chose specially long ago and intended to become true images of His Son, so that His Son might be the eldest of many brothers" (Rom. 8:29).

It is through His Holy Spirit that God makes this "spiritual revolution" possible, allowing our inner man to be conformed also with Christ. ". . .the love of God has been poured into our hearts by the Holy Spirit which has been given us" (Rom. 5:5). The impossible task of bringing our whole being into Christ is possible by the Holy Spirit. He dwells within our bodies and He can subject our various levels of stored up experiences to the healing power of Jesus Christ's love. This is why St. Paul prays for all of us:

> Out of His infinite glory, may He give you the power through
> His Spirit for your hidden self to grow strong, so that Christ
> may live in your hearts through faith, and then, planted in love
> and built on love, you will with all the saints have strength to
> grasp the breadth and the length, the height and the depth;

until, knowing the love of Christ, which is beyond all
knowledge, you are filled with the utter fullness of God
(Ephes. 3:16-19).

Our life is one of "attention" to this world that lies
within us, so that it be renewed, transformed and brought
under the dominion of Jesus Christ. The masters of the
spiritual life, the Fathers of the desert, like St. Paul, had
gone into their "heart" and there did battle to bring the
Kingdom of Christ over every thought, desire, every
movement of their heart.

THE INNER CLOSET

The prayer of the heart begins with the silencing of
the thoughts that are clamoring so loudly within us that
we cannot hear the Word of God speak in the still, silent
voice that Elijah heard on the mountain top (1 Kgs.
19:13). In teaching His apostles how to pray, Jesus Christ
said:

> But when you pray, go to your private room and, when you
> have shut your door, pray to your Father who is in that secret
> place, and your Father who sees all that is done in secret will
> reward you (Matt. 6:6).

St. Dimitri of Rostov (+1709), one of the celebrated
preachers in the history of the Russian Orthodox Church,
gives the common exegesis among the Eastern Fathers
concerning this text. Man is both exterior and interior. St.
Paul refers to this duality in man: ". . .though this outer
man of ours may be falling into decay, the inner man is

renewed day by day" (2 Cor. 4:16). St. Peter preaches that
we should not put too much accent on the outer self,
dressing up for show, putting on fine clothes, but the
important element is how the inner man is adorned.
". . .all this should be inside, in a person's heart, imperish-
able: the ornament of a sweet and gentle disposition — this
is what is precious in the sight of God" (1 Pet. 3:4-5).

It is God alone who can probe the inner depths of
man's heart. He is the one ". . .who probes the inmost
mind and the depths of the heart" (Ps. 64:6). St. Dimitri
likens the inner closet into which we are to enter to pray
deeply in secret before the Heavenly Father to the heart or
mind.

> The closet also is twofold, outer and inner, material and
> spiritual: the material place is of wood or stone, the spiritual
> closet is the heart or mind. St. Theophylact interprets this
> phrase as meaning secret thought or inner vision. Therefore the
> material closet remains always fixed in the same place, but the
> spiritual one you carry about within you wherever you go.
> Wherever man is, his heart is always with him, and so, having
> collected his thoughts inside his heart, he can shut himself in
> and pray to God in secret, whether he be talking or listening,
> whether among few people or many. . . .All that is necessary is
> to raise your mind to God, and descend deep into yourself,
> and this can be done everywhere.[1]

SUBJECTING THE IMAGINATION TO CHRIST

To pray to the Father in the inner sanctuary of our
heart, with the clearest, purest consciousness of His
abiding love and our sincere desire to surrender totally to
Him by a reformed life of love towards others, we must get

rid of any dispersion of inner attention. Love does not grow when we are scattered about in our thoughts, but rather when we are deeply focused and concentrated on the one we love. The heart is where the battlefield is marked off and where victory or defeat is had, where the Kingdom of God will take root or the Kingdom of Darkness.

The hesychastic Fathers saw the necessity of doing battle within the heart that God might be sole possessor of their whole being. For this reason they stressed the psychology of thoughts and the standard teaching of sober vigilance (*nepsis*). We have briefly touched on this important discipline if our inner man is to be healed and brought completely under the dominion of Jesus Christ. We can hear many fervent, emotional sermons from charismatic preachers about turning one's life over to Jesus but we ultimately must return to the "unromantic" asceticism of guarding our hearts and our thoughts so that no enemy can enter and take dominance.

The very early Christians were quite aware of the enemy forces that oppressed them on all sides to gain control of their hearts. St. Peter exhorts the Christians: "Be sober, be vigilant; because your adversary the devil, as a roaring lion, walks about, seeking whom he may devour" (1 Pet. 5:8; KJV). This is not merely Satan, a fallen angel against whom we must battle. It is the whole world, the flesh and the devil that also have found their entrance into our inner life of thought. We have our strength from the Lord from that mastery which His power supplies (Ephes. 6:10-13).

St. Macarius clearly gives the traditional teaching of the saints of the desert, those master psychologists of applied in-depth psychology who for decades refused any other distraction so as to put every inner thought under the complete control of Jesus Christ.

> He who wishes to please God and to wage true enmity against the adversary must wage two wars: one against the visible things of this life which hold us in bondage with their earthly distractions and love for this life and the other war against the affections of sin aroused internally by the hidden spirits of evil. . . .It is possible that if one, in fighting, strips the self from all external, worldly bonds, material things, and carnal pleasures, and begins to adhere to the Lord, he certainly can learn about the war of affections, the internal battle of wicked thoughts. . . .But if he casts off the world, he will find repugnance, his hidden affections, hidden traps, the hidden war, an internal contest. And so begging God, he receives the heavenly arms of the Spirit as St. Paul says (Ephes. 6:14), the breastplate of justice, the helmet of salvation, the shield of faith and the sword of the spirit, God's word. . . .[2]

This is hardly a spirituality for dilettantes. It is for Christ's athletes who have stripped themselves and have entered into the battle, not to give up the fight until Jesus Christ is declared Lord. This struggle never takes a vacation. It goes on at every moment, even in the silence of the night. At all times the Christian knows his weakness and God's strength. God becomes God to him in the battle as he calls upon Him to help him. With the publican he strikes his breast, knowing his own sinfulness: "God, be merciful to me a sinner," (Lk. 18:13) or he cries out continually in the face of his inability to maintain the attack: "Lord, save me!" (Matt. 14:30).

The Holy Spirit breathes into the Christian athlete in battle faith that gives him the strength to be victorious. He knows he is a child of God through the Spirit of Jesus.

With St. John he can be confident because of the Spirit's faith within him assuring him of victory:

> .. .anyone who has been begotten by God
> has already overcome the world;
> this is victory over the world —
> our faith.
> Who can overcome the world?
> Only the man who believes that Jesus is the
> Son of God.. .(1 Jn. 5:4-5).

The warrior soon acquires as a gift from the Spirit of Jesus an inner "eye" which allows him to watch and notice the thoughts as they enter into his heart. Evagrius, one of the master-psychologists among the hesychasts of the 4th century Egyptian desert, likens it to placing a sentinel at the door of one's consciousness who asks each thought: "Are you for the Lord or against Him?" Not only does the heart repel immediately every negative thought that is of the evil one, but more positively the heart gains in the struggle a heart that burns with faith, humility and love. When such heartfelt warmth takes over, the Christian is drawn closer to the Lord Jesus and all other attractions of lesser beauty, lesser enticement, lose their power to allure. Man moves into a state of "passionate indifference" as Teilhard de Chardin calls this openness to the inner Spirit to reveal the way to the Father.

The early Fathers found that it was in the battle that all virtues were attained together. The chief ones of faith, humility and love summarized all the others and if one virtue was not attained, none of them were either. The virtues that came forth were mere signs of a total surrender in love to Jesus Christ as Lord. Therefore, the index of one's healing and submission to Him can be the strength of faith, humility and love that are called forth in the battle. All fear yields ultimately to love. "God's gift was not a spirit of fear, but the Spirit of power and love and self-control. So you are never to be ashamed of witnessing to the Lord. . ." (2 Tim. 1:7-8).

THE POWER OF THE NAME JESUS

Modern Christians can learn from the wise men of the Eastern deserts who found through constant repetition of the name of Jesus the means to remain consciously in the healing presence of Him as Lord of their hearts. It becomes true prayer of the heart only when the pronouncement of the Name is accompanied by a quickening of consciousness of the indwelling Lord. By reverently pronouncing the Name of Jesus the Christian can become present to Him in a powerful experience that is a result of the working of the Holy Spirit to witness to the Kingship of Jesus Christ. By humbly crying out to the presence of Jesus who bears the name that is uttered over and over, the Christian, through the working of the Holy Spirit, begins to experience His presence in a more vital, more real way.

By uttering with fervor of faith, humility and love the sacred name of Jesus, you overcome all enemies lodged within your inner self. You know through the Spirit that you possess within yourself a power that is more powerful than any force for evil, within your unconscious or outside in the world. ". . .Children, you have already overcome these false prophets, because you are from God and you have in you one who is greater than anyone in this world" (1 Jn. 4:4).

By such a constant cry upon the holy name of Jesus,

we remain in the intense awareness of God's all-encompassing love. We are brought to experience the mercy and perfect love of God. By centering upon the Lord Jesus, the areas of darkness within our disturbed psyche are turned into the soft light of His presence, assuring us that we are healed by His strong love. Through such purification we become open still more to receive of God's transforming *agape.* We learn to stand and walk before the Lord at all times. We rely on the Lord for all things. We place all our hopes in Him and in so doing we attain by God's infinite, merciful grace, the fullness of life. The Jesus Prayer in itself does not accomplish these fruits but rather such a continued practice of repeating the name of Jesus disposes us to be open to God's life in us, so that He can create us anew by healing our infirmities through His Spirit dwelling within us.

Jesus Christ will plunge Himself down deeply into our unconscious, into all parts of our mind and heart and take possession of all parts of our being, but only if we cry incessantly that He come and be Lord of our consciousness and even our unconscious. Only then can we be considered true Christians, healed by the loving presence of the Lord Jesus, and free to let Him have total sway over our whole life. "Come, Lord Jesus, Maranatha! Have mercy on me a sinner!"

6

Pray Always

Man is a lonely hunter. He seeks to love and to be loved more ardently, more passionately, with greater, unrelentless striving than any animal seeking food or drink. This is the way God created him — to find himself in relation to other knowing and loving beings. Through such love relationships man is to discover the loving beauty of God.In surrendering to another and ultimately to God in unselfish love, man reaches the highest stage of communication. In such intimate self-giving communion, man expands in a conscious awareness of who he is.

Yet he knows that the awareness of who he is is never a static bit of knowledge. He wants to be more himself as he eagerly seeks to grow in deeper love relationships. Experiencing the sense of identity in love through an expanded state of consciousness, man not only wants more of the same awareness but he cannot live without it. In a way we can say that love is a call to suffer for it means that all lesser desires, above all, all ego-centrism must be put to death. One cannot live now except to love more. Not to love, once he has experienced love, is to tear one's true self into shreds. This is why separation is so painful when a deep level of unity in love has been reached by two persons.

Psychologists like Abraham Maslow have coined the word "peak experience" to describe the "ecstasy" or standing outside of our habitual level of consciousness in a new experience. Children on the playground whirl themselves around and around only to laugh in a light-headed giddiness at being "hyperventilated" beyond their ordinary level of consciousness. As man develops, he discovers other forms of expanding his consciousness. He may find his moments of pushing beyond the "flats" of his ordinary existence to stretch toward his transcendent self in beautiful music, a few martinis before a fire-place with a good book or in stimulating conversation with dear friends. Hallucinogenic drugs, alcohol, surfing, mountain climbing, meditation, sex, the list of ways of expanding our consciousness is seemingly endless.

In all such "methods" the key to pushing ourselves beyond our habitual experience of ourselves toward the world, other persons, God Himself is *concentration*. Being diffused rather than centered scatters our awareness of ourselves as self-positing beings. I like to think of such a state of "return to self" on a deeper level of interiority as not "getting high" but as becoming our true self. We habitually are in a state of "high," far off center, when we are up-tight, filled with choking anxieties, fears, hatred, or simply merely being a victim of indiscriminate reveries. We "come down" by descending into our "heart," that psychic focus-point of our most transcendent self. This inner sanctuary allows our awareness to push to new heights of knowledge and love that lie infinitely beyond the power of our own reason.

Man is not an empty being nor a container to be filled

haphazardly by any and all sense impressions. St. Irenaeus of the 2nd century called man "a receptacle of God's goodness." God pours Himself through His uncreated energies into man, calling him into greater and greater creativity. He stirs within the depths of each man the seeds He planted there in his creation.

AWARENESS OF GOD

Prayer is in its beginning and in its fullest fruition an expansion of our consciousness into an ever-growing awareness that God and we form a union in love. Christian prayer through the faith infused into the one praying by the Spirit of Jesus Christ is an on-going process of discovering not only the abyss that separates the Absolute, all-Holy God from us sinners but also the depths of union that exists between us and God in the very depths of our being. Growth in prayer is therefore a growth in awareness of God, especially as He lives and acts through His infinite love within us. Our response in self-surrendering love pushes our consciousness of our new identity with God to new heights. Something of our past knowledge and experiences in prayer remain. Yet in a way, each time we encounter God in a prayerful experience, because of the increase in awareness, we seem to enter into a fresh, new experience.

Love has that quality of the old, the permanent, the stable and the security and complacency that we enjoy in encountering the same source of beauty and joy. Yet with God above all this sameness and stability of our love for Him fills us with a restless motion, a stretching-out quality towards God, the unpossessable, that thrills us because we know that, try as we may, we can never exhaust this richness. Love always beckons us to partake of more of the joy that is already ours.

If prayer then is man on the deepest level of his being aware of God both within him and without him, then we can imagine how man by nature is a praying-person. Prayer is man's highest fulfillment. It is what he should most naturally enjoy doing. He was made by God for such communication, for such continued expanded conscious-ness of his I-ness in relationship to God's Thou-ness.

God created man to grow into an integrated human being through vital relationships. He is not just a being made up of a body and a soul as two disparate parts. Man is a bodied-being in vital relationship to other bodied beings. He begins the development of his awareness as an *I* through such beginning and enduring relationships. He is also a souled-being in vital relationship with other intel-lectual beings. Still he is called to evolve through growth in consciousness to reach his ultimate transcendence in being a spirited-being in relationship to God's Spirit. All three of these are intimately related and enter into the process of continued growth in identity awareness as man moves from multiplicity into a unity with God through love.

Prayer therefore is not mere conversation in words with God. It is more than a striving to attain a "nice," pleasant feeling. Ultimately it is a "look" upon God, a loving gaze that God's silent gaze of love, His Holy Spirit, infuses into us, or better, evolves as a seed lying in readiness in the spiritual powers of our consciousness. I have defined contemplation in these words:

> It is a human being standing, as it were, outside of the habitual idea that he has of himself, the person that he thinks he is. It is

his getting down below that false everyday ego and getting into his deepest source where he stands before God, consciously turning toward his Source, his Origin. Here we can see we are not dealing with an exercise of piety alone. We are certainly not dealing with anything that is dependent upon perseverance in a certain method. But contemplation is something applicable to every human being, and therefore should be as natural as a baby looking on his father or mother's face.[1]

My prayer is more total, more human and also more divine, the more consciously I can be aware of my I-ness and at the same of God's Other-ness, His Thou-ness. The thrust of my whole Christian life should therefore be towards a constant living in that keen awareness that is ever opening up to an expansion in consciousness of God's presence to me and my being present to Him.

Jesus Christ teaches us today as He did in His life-time that we are to live in this state of awareness, of constant prayer: "Watch you, therefore, and pray always . . . ." (Lk. 21:36; KJV). "Then Jesus told them a parable about the need to pray continually and never lose heart" (Lk. 18:1). St. Paul exhorts the early Christians "never to cease praying" (1 Thess. 5:17). When we read the Apostolic Fathers' writings, we find that there were fixed times to pray to the Lord. But each Christian also realized in a way far different from us that it was his privilege, it was the meaning of his Christian life, to stand before the Lord in constant awareness of God's presence and adore Him as man's Creator and loving Father by all that he did or thought or said. "Whatever you eat, whatever you drink, whatever you do at all, do it for the glory of God" (1 Cor. 10:31).

But how can we pray always? If the early Christians achieved any type of constant awareness, one thing is certain. Their lives were lived on a much simpler level without the great anxieties that cloud our daily lives. One has to spend so much psychic energy just to concentrate on the speed and noise, often the violence and recklessness of power-driven machines around us in order to stay alive with little time left over for quiet, prayerful absorption in God. Many of us would enjoy nothing better than to spend hours each day in loving adoration of God, but we know that God is asking us to roll up our sleeves and get on with the development of His world.

"IF YOU WISH TO HAVE A PART WITH ME. . ."

Jesus had often told His listeners as He tells us that if we want to enter into an intimacy with Him and His Heavenly Father, we must first desire this intimacy. It lies therefore not in any one act of piety or method or prayers said, but it is more importantly a state of desiring to be one with God in all of our affections, in all that we do, think and say. Incessant prayer, the goal of the prayer of the heart, should be a possibility for all true Christians. It really depends upon our willingness to live in that state of conscious-relationship with God. It is an attitude of "being" always toward God, pushing our consciousness (not necessarily our concentration) in the direction of God as our Ultimate Concern.

Inwardness or the state of praying unceasingly is primarily the loving surrender of our whole being into the loving hands of God. God's Holy Spirit alone is able to effect this. It lies within the capacity ultimately of man's own willing. Yet his will is "converted" unto the Lord by the gentle drawing of the Spirit's gift of faith. It is the "Yes, Father," uttered constantly within the human consciousness of Jesus Christ as He lived out His life, moment by moment.

Such a faith instills a child-like trust (among the Greek Fathers this was called: *parrhesia*), whereby we can let go of our lives. One of the greatest difficulties preventing such constant living in the remembrance of God is the multiplicity of our anxieties and desires outside of God's loving providence. Jesus insists that we must not be over-solicitous about our lives, what we are to eat, wear, etc. Our Heavenly Father who takes care of the birds of the field and clothes the lilies of the field in such beauteous array, will He not also take care of us? (Matt. 6:26-30; Lk. 12:22-32).

We can lift the greatest weight from our spirits by trusting in God to provide for all of our needs. This providential, loving concern touches all details of our lives, even the most banal. We can see already how prayer as a constant state of being before God the Father is intimately connected with our daily life and with each event in that life. Everything then is seen as a gift, coming down from the Father of lights (James 1:17). Nothing is boring, negative, meaningless before such a penetrating faith that pierces through man's "carnal" way of looking at events to come into touch with a higher wisdom, the knowledge of God's love given us by the Holy Spirit.

> The Spirit Himself and our spirit bear united witness that we are children of God. And if we are children we are heirs as well: heirs of God and coheirs with Christ, sharing His sufferings so as to share His glory (Rom. 8:16-17).

A loving surrender in all things to God's loving guidance comes from the Christian's belief that all things really work unto good to those who love the Lord (Rom. 8:28). Even sufferings become a part of prayerful union with the loving Father who, like the vinedresser, prunes us whom He loves in order that we might bring forth more fruit (Jn. 15:1-2). The Holy Spirit alone can teach us to pray incessantly and part of this constancy in prayer comes through the Holy Spirit's infusion of faith and knowledge to see with different eyes, those of the spirit.

> These are the very things that God has revealed to us through the Spirit, for the Spirit reaches the depths of everything, even the depths of God. After all, the depths of a man can only be known by his own spirit, not by any other man, and in the same way the depths of God can only be known by the Spirit of God. Now instead of the spirit of the world, we have received the Spirit that comes from God, to teach us to understand the gifts that He has given us. . . .A spiritual man, on the other hand, is able to judge the value of everything, and his own value is not to be judged by other men. . .But we are those who have the mind of Christ (1 Cor. 2:10-16).

SOME INSIGHTS FROM THE FATHERS

If we turn to the early Fathers of the Church we can gain some very important insights about living in the consciousness of God perpetually and thus praying incessantly. These Fathers were mystics, men of great purity of heart, asceticism, great absorption in God and were bent on teaching the faithful the most essential elements in Christianity. For them this doctrine of praying always or

how a Christian could maintain a constant r<
love of God was one of maximum importanc

It was Origen in the 3rd century wh
essential difference between actual absorption in concentrated prayer and praying always by having a will in
conformity to that of God's will. If prayer is essentially an
elevation or raising of the mind towards God, then what
determines the "prayerfulness" of our actual praying
moments or our actions done in a prayerful attitude, for
Origen, is that both be done for the love of God.[2]

Aphraates, the Syrian mystic and theologian of the
4th century, shows how purity of heart is more than a
state as Evagrius and Cassian taught (a psychological and
experimental state). He teaches simply: "Do what is
pleasing to God; this is what prayer is." The basis for
making all actions pleasing to God is faith. Without faith,
Aphraates claims, man cannot be pleasing to God. Faith
embraces hope and love. It is what gives the heart the
purity or direction to God as man's ultimate goal. It is
faith that convinces man, by God's infused gift of new
knowledge, that God is man's Master and worthy of all
submission and loving service.

It would be up to the individual to determine the
times of formal prayer which would be of utmost necessity
if man were to pray continually in all he did to please God.
But man had to purify his heart by seeking to do all his
works to please God.

It is St. Augustine who develops in the most complete
and concise manner the solid doctrine of how a Christian
can pray always and still concentrate on his daily tasks. In
his famous letter to Proba he teaches that incessant prayer
is possible by man's directing all of his actions toward the
good pleasure of God. "Hence it is in faith, hope and

charity that we pray with a perpetual desire of doing so."[3]

St. Thomas was greatly influenced by Augustine's doctrine when he declared that the cause of prayer is the desire of charity; it is from it, that is, from this desire that prayer must proceed. Such a desire in us must be continuous either actually or virtually. The power of such a desire remains in us in everything that we do out of charity. It is St. Paul's injunction to do all things for the glory of God (1 Cor. 10:31).

So we see that for Origen, Aphraates and Augustine it is commonly taught that all Christians must pray unceasingly. But to do so does not mean only to concentrate on formal prayer. Some periods must be set aside for this total absorption in God in thanksgiving and praise of Him from whom come all gifts to mankind. But praying in between these formal periods is accomplished by having an intention through faith, hope and love to seek always to please God and accomplish His holy will. This is what it means ultimately to have a pure heart and to see God in all things. The heart of man is a good treasure which brings forth good things (Matt. 12:35). And the "good things" is the constant desire to love God in all actions, thoughts, words.

One of the greatest Christian psychologists, most shrewd in his observances of the workings of the human psyche, especially as it unfolds in this constant awareness of God, is Evagrius of Pontus of the 4th century. He insists that man should be able to determine from how he reacts during his dreams how much healing of the psyche has taken place through constant remembrance of God. In dreams, says Evagrius, the soul reacts to the images of the dreams according to profound dispositions that might be covered over in broad-daylight consciousness. When the

Christian reaches a complete immersion in God, he will not even have passionate reactions in his dreams, let alone not having such in his full conscious moments.

St. Basil the Great gives the most practical, concrete synthesis that goes beyond the intellectualism of Evagrius and Cassian. The two latter insist on incessant prayer by way of either a complete purification of the mind of all images and thoughts, as Evagrius teaches in his treatise on prayer, or as Cassian insists, on a monologistic prayer, a Christian mantra repeated as a fixation upon the presence of God. Basil sees that man cannot, especially the busy person in the world and even the monk who lives to help his neighbor in his social needs, concentrate continually in such explicit turnings to the Lord. What is needed, he insists on, is an attitude of mind whereby man seeks always to obey the word of God and to do His will. This comes down to what he calls "the remembrance or thought of God."

In a negative way Basil writes in his *Long Rules*: "We must free our mind from all the worries of the world and keep it away entirely from everything that could bring us dissipation and distraction" (5th Question). It is within the power of man to control negative thoughts that divert man's attention or consciousness of God's dominating love and providential care over all details of man's life. When man forgets this by becoming absorbed in the cares of this world he really is living a lie; he refuses to live according to the truth, that we have a loving Father who takes care of us as His children.

But more positively Basil sees that man must strive to remain in the consciousness of God's presence.

Having complied with this obligation, we must watch over our
heart with all possible care, and not allow the thought of God
to vanish or the remembrance of His marvelous deeds be
defiled by the phantoms of vain and useless things; but,
wherever we may be, we must always bear with us the holy
thought of the majesty of God engraved in the innermost part
of our souls as an ineffaceable seal, by means of a most pure
and continual remembrance of His divine perfections.[4]

This brings us to the real issue that haunts so many
sincere Christians. Can we pray always in our thought? Is
not action done out of love for God the real index of our
true love for God and neighbor? But how can we do such
loving actions if we do not think of God? For St. Basil,
who of all the early Greek Fathers was the most pragmatic
and in my opinion the one who best had pulled it all
together, better than most of the intellectual monks living
in the desert like Evagrius, the remembrance or thought of
God was more than a thought that "purified" our
intention before we jumped into some action. It is, to use
Teilhard de Chardin's phrase, a divine milieu that permeates, influences, guides and determines everything we
do.

It comes down to what has been earlier said, a
focusing, a centering in faith, hope and love upon God as
our Ultimate Concern. Our heart is pure when we in our
consciousness have God as the motivating force behind all
of our actions. It is of value to quote a bit at length from
the reasonableness of this great teacher of the spiritual life,
St. Basil:

> . . .we should watch over our heart with all vigilance not only
> to avoid ever losing the thought of God or sullying the
> memory of His wonders by vain imaginations, but also in order

to carry about the holy thoughts of God stamped upon our souls as an ineffaceable seal by continuous and pure recollection. . .so the Christian directs every action, small and great, according to the will of God, performing the action at the same time with care and exactitude, and keeping his thoughts fixed upon the One who gave him the work to do. In this way, he fulfills the saying, 'I set the Lord always in my sight; for He is at my right hand, that I be not moved' and he also observes the precept, 'Whether you eat or drink or whatsoever else you do, do all to the glory of God.' . . .We should perform every action as if under the eyes of the Lord and think every thought as if observed by Him. . .fulfilling the words of the Lord: 'I seek not my own will but the will of Him that sent me, the Father.'[5]

Thus incessant prayer means praying.in the heart. It means being made conscious of the ever-abiding presence of God through the power of the Holy Spirit infusing into us faith, hope and charity in order that we can measure all our thoughts, words and deeds according to the loving will of the Father so that in all things we can please Him.

"ATTEND TO YOURSELF"

Total obedience to the will of God expressed by His commands and wishes through the delicate inspirations of the Holy Spirit is accomplished only at a great cost of consciously turning within oneself and reflecting on what God is asking of oneself at any given time. This, for St. Basil again, means that God has placed in man, not in any other animals of His creation, the ability not merely to remember God through knowledge as the goal of man's life, but more in particular to be able to direct and guide man's actions towards God. To do this there is need of continual control over our attention, our consciousness and a guard over our thoughts.

This is the demanding doctrine of the early Fathers on *nepsis* or "sober vigilance" over the flow of consciousness and every thought that enters into that consciousness. St. Hesychius of Jerusalem insisted that it is impossible to please God and be free of sin without the guarding of the mind and living in the purity of heart.[6]

The mind must live in this reverence due to God and have confidence in Him so as to do all to please God and not for self. This is to submit each thought and feeling and motive for doing each action so as to put them in harmony with God's will. This is to fulfill the one great commandment to be true to God's word. Then Jesus Christ and His Father will come and abide in that man (Jn. 14:23-24). In this way the Christian will be able to pray incessantly. It will not be so much by a constant thought, not even the Jesus Prayer repeated uninterruptedly within man, but it will be the directing power of man's will to want to remain in the continued remembrance of God's presence that makes it an accomplished fact. If man does not have this continued desire, this "passionate indifference" to quote again Teilhard de Chardin, to wait on the will of God, then no amount of prayers and no amount of works will be pleasing to God. This is the directing force involved in true love. The only valid "remembrance of God" is that which directs man in all of his thoughts, words and actions to be the person God wishes him to be in those circumstances. He is given by God's Spirit the gift to be totally centered upon God in his consciousness and never to move away from the dictating control of God's will.

"GIVING THANKS ALWAYS"

One reason why we do not remain in the "remembrance" of God is that we become dissipated and fail to give thanks to God for all His gifts. If our faith and hope and love for God are keen and vibrant, functioning throughout the whole day, then we will be able to see God's goodness in every event, in every creature that passes our path. Praise to God will be constantly on our lips and in our hearts because our inner vision shows us the loving presence and activity of God operating continually in our lives. St. Paul tells us: "Be happy at all times; pray constantly; and for all things give thanks to God, because this is what God expects you to do in Christ Jesus" (1 Thess. 5:18).

We may thank God in some occasions and thus enter into a state of prayer. But to thank God in all things, above all, in the dark moments, those events that crush us and seemingly tell us that the powers of evil are all around us and nearly victorious, when God seems so absent, this requires faith and a dying to our own limited vision of reality. It means to "live in our heart" by living on a greater conscious level of God's *being-toward* me.

This does not mean that we ignore the "gut reactions" that we might be having. To die is not natural; for we have been made by God to go forth in a great openness to embrace life in all of its manifestations. Anything that poses to us a threat of death to us on any level becomes an object of fear and avoidance. Jesus did not really want to die when He prayed in the Garden of Gethsemane that His Father take away from Him the impending death on the cross. It is through attention, through a conscious reflection that we learn to rise above our "natural," even sinful,

ways of looking at things to put on the mind of Jesus
Christ. Only His Spirit can infuse into our broken hearts
the knowledge that can reconcile at the same time this
"not-wanting" this cross and our "wanting" it if this is a
part of our Heavenly Father's providence.

This is not stoic resignation. It is not a naive ignoring
of pain or a belief that God is causing all our pains and
sufferings. We are unable in any given moment to discern
completely what God wills and what He permits. But true
Christian acceptance of God's presence in our lives, hence
the possibility of true prayer at all times, is to realize that
God will be faithful as Father to us in each moment as we
open ourselves to encounter Him in the concrete circumstances of the present "now."

St. Basil came to grips with this problem in writing
about a mother that had recently lost her little child
through death. His words are full of Christian wisdom and
help us to understand our quest for incessant prayer.

> Let the will of God cohabit with your will; like a light which
> penetrates everything by its rays, it will be there without
> interruption to bring you to pass an accurate judgment on
> things. Way back in advance it sees to it that your soul is
> protected, it prepares the true ideas concerning every event,
> and will not allow you to lose your bearings, whatever may
> happen. Your mind having previously been trained will meet
> with the unshakable and steady strength of a rock by the
> seashore the furious onslaughts of winds and surging waves.[7]

St. Paul realized also that his sufferings were occasions of his being tested. "These sufferings bring patience,
as we know, and patience brings perseverance, and
perseverance brings hope, and this hope is not deceptive,

because the love of God has been poured into our hearts by the Holy Spirit who has been given us" (Rom. 5:3-5).

PRAYING INCESSANTLY IS POSSIBLE

To turn within and pray incessantly by living in an awareness given us by the Holy Spirit of God's immense love for us guiding us in all things is possible for all of us. It requires, however, a constant living out of our Baptism, a crossing over from our own self-containment and a putting on of Jesus Christ's mind of seeking always to please the Heavenly Father. Praying always is a state of not saying prayers but a state of standing before God in the depths of our being and being constantly in tune with His operations. We find ourselves therefore less distracted by the fears of what others would say, of norms and fashions set by a worldly society or persons close to us. We even can rise from the haunting memories of our sinful past and our crippling "mind-set" patterns of thoughts and images to a freedom and clarity of inner vision that Jesus Christ had promised would be the possession of His disciples who heard His word.

Such sensitivity to God's presence in our lives awakens us to His beauty in the world around us. We seem to drink deeper of the natural beauties. We smell the rose with deeper joy, praise God for its delicate unfolding petals. We become more humbly grateful for all that God brings into our lives of beauty, goodness, above all, of love. We reverence His presence in the human loves that we are privileged to receive from others and we wish to serve Him in bringing those friends into the fullness of happiness and perfection as God should wish.

Gratitude is constant in our lives. Hence we find ourselves bursting out spontaneously in praise of God for His abundant goodness towards us. This was the state of St. Paul that he wished for all Christians: "Be filled with the Spirit. Sing the words and tunes of the psalms and hymns when you are together and go on singing and chanting to the Lord in your hearts, so that always and everywhere you are giving thanks to God who is our Father in the name of our Lord Jesus Christ" (Ephes. 5:18-20).

Prayer then becomes no longer a thing to do but the Spirit begins to pray within us by the praise we have and the thanks we give to God in all things. It is only the Holy Spirit who can make incessant prayer possible. For, again, as St. Paul says:

> The Spirit too comes to help us in our weakness. For when we cannot choose words in order to pray properly, the Spirit Himself expresses our plea in a way that could never be put into words and God who knows everything in our hearts knows perfectly well what He means, and that the pleas of the saints expressed by the Spirit are according to the mind of God. We know that by turning everything to their good God co-operates with all those who love Him, with all those that He has called according to His purpose (Rom. 8:26-28).

This Holy Spirit has infused into us a spirit of contemplation so that no longer is there a distinction between our prayer and our action. Our whole life with all of its details is a prayer of praise and thanksgiving to God. For such a Christian there can never be true solitude since his inner vision by the power of the Spirit reveals the loving presence of God in all things. Everything is impregnated by God's caressing love. All things call us towards God who lives deeply within us. He is not only immanently present within our "hearts" but we can find Him easily enough as the immanent presence within all other persons and things, in all events.

Everywhere our faith reveals to us the unity of all things within the omnipresence and omnipotence of God. Prayer incessantly is that state of living totally in God and for God and through God. There will be an ever-increasing craving for moments to be alone with God in total surrender. Yet every action will be the occasion also of living out that surrender given in concentrated prayer. In a way we can say that unless there are such moments of deep absorption in God our centering in the present moment of each "now" would be shaky and weak. The early Fathers give us another insight as to how we can pray incessantly. That is their insistence on fixed moments of withdrawal to be alone with God on a deep level of surrendering love to His inner presence. Let us explore their insistence on praying deeply, especially at night, when the mind is quiet. It is a microcosmic death that makes the other deaths through the day in all of our many activities possible and that leads us ever to a greater sharing even now in the oneness with Christ, in a resurrection into greater unity with Him in whom, by whom and for whom we have all been made.

7

Tears and Enlightenment

Man is superior to all other creatures on the face of the earth insofar as he can search out and find new meaning for his life. He can "go beyond," transcending his present state of life by stretching upward through his powers of intellection and willing to become more united with God, his Absolute Meaning.

To begin this process of *metanoia*, or returning to man's true self, which means also to return more consciously toward God, man must begin by an honest look at his existential place in time, his being-in-the world as "thrown," "factical" and inauthentic.[1] The hard shell of self-containment or pride must be split by a new knowledge given by God that is called *humility*. Humility is grace given by God on two levels of enlightenment. The first derives from man's brokenness as he is filled with a sense of self-abasement, shame, fear, "ontological anxiety" (Heidegger's *Angst*).

Dr. John Macquarrie well defines this beginning stirring in man's being to be other than he now is.

. . .that basic tension or malaise which is, perhaps somewhat misleadingly, called usually "anxiety" (Angst), the sense of the precariousness of an existence that any moment may cease to exist. What is disclosed in this mood (as in other moods, and in sensuous intuition) can be brought to expression in words, when we attain explicit awareness of the finite and transient character of the existence of a self-in-the-world. Yet the very attainment of such an awareness is also a transcending of mere transience, and is the awakening of the quest for grace and meaning.[2]

The working of God's grace to instill into man an anxiety, fear, disgust as he confronts his existence in the light of its "non-being" is not merely a reflection on death and a cry for immortality. It is an ontological "nostalgia" to leave the "husks of swine" and return to man's true self which is to be in love with his Heavenly Father. It is the soft dew of God's grace falling upon the hard desert floor of man's heart to stir the seeds planted there in man's being made "according to the image and likeness" of God.

St. Symeon the New Theologian captures this first phase of God's enlightenment — humility, in somewhat dramatic imagery.

Likewise that soul about which I am speaking,
when it sees how the light shines
and knows that itself is completely in most terrible darkness
and in this completely enclosed prison
of most profound ignorance,
then it sees just where it is lying,
where it is locked in
and that this place is completely a mud hole,
full of slimy, poisonous snakes;
that it itself is chained,

both hands and feet bound by shackles
and that it is covered with dust and filth;
that it is also wounded
from the bites of the reptiles
and that its own flesh is puffed up
and also covered with numerous worms.
Seeing this, how will the soul not shudder?
How will it not weep?
And how will it not cry out?
And ardently be repentant and beg to be rescued
from such terrible fetters?
Yes, all who see such
indeed will lament and groan
and will want to follow after Christ
who makes the light so radiant! (Hymn 30)[3]

Man stands facing himself and his broken world. He can let Divine Love burn out the impurities and allow himself to transcend his imprisonment to stretch toward the Infinite. Or he can burn in his own locked-in, gin-soaked Hell that Camus describes in *The Fall*.

T. S. Eliot in his poem, *Little Gidding*, has expressed this descent of God's Spirit of Love falling into man's broken spirit to stir him to a purifying repentance and greater transcendence or to remain hopelessly burning within one's sinfulness.

The dove descending breaks the air
With flame of incandescent terror
of which the tongues declare
The one discharge from sin and error.
The only hope, or else despair
Lies in the choice of pyre or pyre
To be redeemed from fire by fire.

Who then devised the torment? Love.
Love is the unfamiliar Name
Behind the hands that wove
The intolerable shirt of flame
Which human power cannot remove.
We only live, only suspire
Consumed by either fire or fire.

CENTERED UPON GOD

The second aspect of humility is the positive enlightenment that results when man yields to God's grace in his
brokenness and begins to live a new life-in-God. This
aspect of humility is what Bernard Lonergan defines as a
true religious conversion — "...the type of consciousness
that deliberates, makes judgments of value, decides, acts
responsibly and freely."[4]

This opting to live responsibly is to love God in all
things. It is to be maximally conscious of His supremacy in
our lives and to direct all our thoughts and actions toward
Him in loving submission. But before we can reach this
second phase of humility as a constant state of conscious
loving God as Father, the Spirit must pour continually into
our hearts the sense of brokenness and sinfulness.

This is what the Fathers of the desert called *penthos*,
an abiding sense of our "separateness" from God. Through
reflection on this state of incompleteness in the light of
God's loving mercy and the nearness of death, the
Christian is able to reach by the gift of the Holy Spirit a
state of conversion that makes the total penitent break
down in tears. To weep tears of purification was a duty for
anyone serious about greater union with God through

mystical contemplation. It was a sign of a complete "cracking" of the false-ego, moving one into new enlightenment and which would be confirmed by the state of constant joyful humility, incessant living consciously out of love for God that we have been calling the "prayer of the heart."

Let me give two examples of tears connoting a higher expansion of consciousness and enlightenment.

A friend of mine has been working for the past year with a Zen Buddhist Roshi. Reporting to him the success he had been having with the repetition of the *koan* given him by his master, he was told: "Until I see you on the floor, your face bathed completely in tears, I will not believe that you have broken into the inner meaning of that koan."

That remark reminded me of a description given by John C. Lilly in his book, *The Center of the Cyclone:*

> As I watched the sunset the second evening, I suddenly saw a three-layered cloud formation over the Pacific Ocean of extreme brilliance and immense beauty with a vertical shaft of brilliant white light. The formation was a triple cross. I started to cry, lonely at first, for me. I went with the grief. It changed to grief-joy combined and it was for all humans, first on this planet, later throughout the galaxy. This crying "+12" continued through three days including a visit by Oscar. During his visit, I did not shut down the crying or the grief-joy and shared it with him. Later he called this a special region, 'making the Christ, the green qutub' in state +12.[5]

TEARS AMONG THE FATHERS OF THE DESERT

I would like to present in this chapter the teaching of the athletes of the early centuries of Christianity who fled to the deserts of Egypt, Syria, Mesopotamia in order to enter into their "center of the Cyclone." There is a consistent doctrine among these Fathers, the Christian gurus. And included in this common doctrine is the insistence that without tears that pour profusely for days on end there is no true enlightenment.

The Fathers stress the difference between what the individual must do to dispose himself for the coming of this gift and the gratuitous gift from God. The monk must maintain a general compunction and interior weeping that come under the ascetical practices aimed to keep the soul in a constant frame of grief. But when the gift comes, it breaks on the soul suddenly like a "flood leaping over all the dikes set up by sin; the other type of compunction falls on the soul like rain onto the grass."[6]

God's grace moves us with a warming of our heart and makes our whole soul glad with an ineffable, inflaming love for God and man, enlightening the mind and pouring out into our interior feelings of great joy. Then tears pour out even without our own willing them and they spurt forth without effort on our part. John Climacus says that the soul then is like a baby. It weeps and is physically affected, that is, "the spirit rejoices and expresses this joy even on its face. God grant us these tears."[7]

Nil Sorsky (+1508), who brought this teaching of hesychastic enlightenment from Mount Athos to Russia, describes the common teaching of all the early Fathers of the desert:

> There are some who have not attained completely this gift of tears, but find it; some through contemplating the secret beauties of the Architect and Lover of mankind, God; others through reading the lives of the Saints and their teachings;

others by the Jesus Prayer; others come to this compunction from certain prayers, composed by Saints; others pray some canons and tropars; others through remembrance of their sins; others from the remembrance of death and judgment; others through longing for the future joys of Heaven, and so by various ways, they obtain the gift of tears. If anyone by any such subject is aroused to tears, he must meditate on how to retain this weeping until the tears no longer come; for one, wishing to be delivered from sins, is delivered from them by weeping and one, wishing to keep the self from sin, is kept so by weeping, said the Fathers.[8]

NEED TO PRAY FOR THIS GIFT

The continuous doctrine of all the early Fathers, especially of Evagrius, is that one must pray continually to receive this gift which alone was the proof that man had broken onto a new level of understanding himself in relation to God and to the rest of the world around him. Evagrius summarizes in a few short words the theology of tears that would thereafter be repeated by all who followed the spirituality of the desert in their search for higher contemplation or enlightenment. "Before all else, pray to be given tears, that weeping may soften the savage hardness which is in your soul and, having acknowledged your sin unto the Lord (Ps. 31,5), you may receive from Him the remission of sins."[9]

The common teaching on the need to pray for tears was accepted also in the Roman West. St. Gregory, Pope of Rome, insists also on asking God for this precious gift of tears:

> Who does good works and has been deemed worthy to have received some gifts from God, but has not yet received tears, he must pray for this in order to weep, either thinking about the last judgment or longing for the heavenly kingdom or repenting over evil past deeds or kneeling before the Cross of Christ, seeing Him suffering for us, our Crucified Savior. [10]

Ephrem the Syrian, Germanos, patriarch of Constantinople, John Damascene, Symeon the New Theologian, Isaac the Syrian (the most famous teacher of the theology of tears), all insist on the necessity of crying out with bruised soul to God for this necessary gift without which the soul will neither be washed from its past iniquities, nor leave completely such passionate desires to cling only to God.

Isaac insists vigorously that, "So long as you have not reached the realm of tears, that which is hidden within you still serves the world, that is, you still lead a worldly life and do the work of God only with your outer man, while the inner man is barren; for his fruit begins with tears.[11]

Tears were a true indication that the mind was leaving the prison of this world and entering into a new age. Tears flow because the birth of the spiritual child is at hand, grace is about to bring forth the Divine Image into the light of the life to come.[12]

Again Isaac speaks of these mystical tears that are a state of a new level of being:

> I am speaking of tears such as flow unceasingly day and night. The eyes of a man who has reached this degree become like a spring of water for up to two years and more, after which he comes to the stilling of thoughts. After the stilling of thoughts, as far as nature permits it in part, there comes that tranquillity which St. Paul mentions (Hebr. 4,3) and here the mind begins to contemplate mysteries.[13]

PREPARATION FOR THE GIFT

On the one hand, the Fathers taught that the gift of tears was gratuitously given by God. Yet on the other hand, they did not conceive it as reserved for a few "gifted" mystics. All hermits in the desert wept for sins for no other reason than that they wanted to do so and they wanted so because they believed it their duty. It was a duty enjoined upon them if they were serious about advancing in contemplation. They had to bring the healing power of the Risen Lord into their hellish inner-world, to expose the dark regions under Satan to the light of a new understanding of their true nature.[14]

Still one must take precaution not to war against nature, forcing it to weep physically when it cannot. Symeon the New Theologian cautions against forcing the body to accomplish a thing that is above its strength, for weakness will ensue.[15] Still Symeon also repeats from the Fathers of the desert, from Gregory of Nyssa through Evagrius, John Chrysostom, Theodore Studite, Barsanuphius, Climacus and all the Sinaite Fathers: "If our soul is in such a disposition, i.e. really understands its true nature and its actual fallen state and is hence filled with deep sorrow and compunction at its estrangement from God, it cannot but weep bitterly with tears."[16]

St. Gregory of Nyssa simply states the case: "It is impossible for one to live without tears who considers things exactly as they really are. . ."[17]

Part of considering things as they really are was to consider death, the inclinations of one's fallen nature through past sins (Jung's false ego) and the "disobedience of Adam" towards the things of sense perception and away from union with God. Such deep reflection of the inner world of imprisonment would fill the soul with compunction and interior grief. There would also be engendered in the deepest way possible an accompanying hunger to be other than the prisoner in bonded exile. There would be the stretching forth of Gregory Nyssa's *epectasis*.

This desire to be penetrated with as deep a sorrow as possible before the goodness of God was the important feature to be stressed. The interior desire in itself was a spiritual weeping that opened the inner powers of the soul so that such interior weeping would turn to physical tears as a gift of God when man reached an intense and abiding sense of compunction. The gift of tears, it should be noted, never was sought for itself, but only as a criterion that a person had undergone a great sorrow, regret, fear of losing the most precious possession in life.

EFFECTS OF TEARS: ENLIGHTENMENT

Tears were powerful and one should, according to the teaching of the Fathers, seek to remain in such a state of weeping, for such tears have great power and action in destroying and uprooting sins and passions, anything that is an obstacle to enter into one's true nature. Isaac the Syrian describes the benefits of tears as more excellent than all other gifts through which we come to purity of heart and are made worthy of all other spiritual gifts.[18]

Ephrem describes the effects of tears as "enlightening the heart. . .the fires of retribution for my sins may be extinguished by this simple weeping."[19] Symeon the New Theologian gives another reason for the necessity of shedding constant tears:

Clean the stains of my soul and give me tears of penance, loving tears out of love, tears of salvation, tears that clean the darkness of my mind, making me light so that I may see You, Light of the world, Enlightenment to my repentant eyes.[20]

Throughout all patristic literature the image of tears as a second Baptism is most frequently found. Tears remit sins and regenerate Divine Life in the soul. Climacus set it down definitively for all successors:

Greater than Baptism itself is the fountain of tears after Baptism, even though it is somewhat audacious to say so. For Baptism is the washing away of evils that were in us before, but sins committed after Baptism are washed away by tears. As Baptism is received in infancy we have all defiled it, but we cleanse it anew with tears. And if God in His love for mankind had not given us tears, few indeed and hard to find would be those in the state of grace.[21]

Hence we see the great effects of tears as purifying the soul from sin and the attractions of passions towards evil; also tears illuminate the dark recesses of the soul to bring it under the light of Christ's teaching and powerful healing.

Thus purified, the contemplative can listen to the promptings of the Holy Spirit within and perform all in harmony with the mind of God. Tears give the mind a deeper knowledge of God and of oneself. This illumination received through tears "enlightens the mind and pours out into our interior a deep feeling of joy. . .then the battle with the enemy becomes easier and temptations are quelled and calmed. . .from the depths of the heart pours a certain ineffable sweetness, reacting on the whole body and on every sick and diseased sense with an exulting joy."[22]

One of the great evident effects from tears that flowed from the calm and peace experienced is the joy that radiates over the whole being of the newly enlightened. Christ had promised this to His disciples after they would have endured suffering and persecution for His sake. "Rejoice and be glad, for a rich reward awaits you in Heaven." But the monks in the desert knew that Heaven was not a place, but a state of interiority, a vision of enlightenment that placed them in a state higher than the unenlightened who did not dare to "go over to the other side" within the cave of their being. St. Antony, the father of all Christian hermits who dared to launch out into the desert, is described by Athanasius in his biography of Antony as a person possessing unruffled calm and a radiant joy that shone from within his inner self.

> ...For as his soul was free from disturbances, his outward appearance was calm; so from the joy of his soul he possessed a cheerful countenance, and from his bodily movement could be perceived the condition of his soul, as it is written: 'When the heart is merry, the countenance is cheerful, but when it is sorrowful, it is cast down' (Prov. 15,13). ...Thus Antony was recognized; he was never disturbed for his soul was at peace; he was never downcast for his mind was joyous.[23]

RE-INTEGRATION

More than giving to the Christian a constant, unperturbed joy, the gift of tears brings about a searing awareness of the presence of the Holy Spirit who as light and fire divinizes man made "according to the Image and Likeness" of God, that is Jesus Christ. Symeon the New Theologian describes this movement from tears to a divinizing enlightenment in these words:

> If a man, who possesses within him the light of the Holy Spirit, is unable to bear its radiance, he falls prostrate on the ground and cries out in great fear and terror, as one who sees and experiences something beyond nature, above words or reason. He is then like a man whose entrails have been set on fire and, unable to bear the scorching flame, he is utterly devastated by it and deprived of all power to be in himself. But, through constant watering and cooling by tears, the flame of Divine desire in him burns all the brighter, producing yet more copious tears, and being washed by their flow he shines with ever-greater' radiance. And, when the whole of him is aflame and he becomes as light, the words of John the Divine are fulfilled: 'God unites with gods and is know by them.'[24]

It was the great teacher of the doctrine of tears, Isaac the Syrian, who more concretely described the gift of tears as the sign of a new birth that comes after a long purification. He distinguishes between tears that come intermittently in the performance of the spiritual exercises and tears that flow unceasingly day and night up to two years and more.[25] There follows then the quieting of all thoughts and man has entered into the state of *apatheia*, passionlessness or the tranquillity and integration of all his senses, emotions and faculties. It is then that the Holy Spirit infuses the highest gifts of contemplation. Permit me to give a final citation from Isaac who clearly links up the gift of tears with the highest state of re-integration or infused contemplation.

When you reach the realm of tears, then know that your mind has left the prison of this world, has put its foot on the path of a new age and has begun to smell the scent of new and wondrous air. Tears begin to flow because the birth of the spiritual child is near. Grace, the common mother of all, wishes mysteriously to bring forth a divine image into the light of the life to come. But these tears are of a different order from those which come from time to time to those practising silence (sometimes during contemplation, sometimes during reading or at the time of prayer). I am not speaking of this type of tears, but of such as flow unceasing day and night.

The eyes of a man who has reached this degree become like a spring of water for up to two years and more after which he comes to the stilling of thoughts. After the stilling of thoughts, as far as nature permits it in part, there comes that *rest* of which St. Paul speaks (Heb. 4,3). In this peaceful tranquillity the mind begins to contemplate mysteries. Then the Holy Spirit begins to reveal to him heavenly things—and God comes to dwell in him and resurrects in him the fruit of the Spirit. When you enter the realm of stillness of thoughts, the profusion of tears is taken from you—and tears come to you in moderation and at the proper time.[26]

Thus the gift of tears lasts for a definite period of time during which the flow of tears is incessant. When this continuous weeping ceases, the contemplative enters into a new stage of enlightenment, that is characterized by the stilling of all thoughts and a more total infusion of God's knowledge.

We can summarize what has been said by the simple statement that, for the Christian seeking enlightenment, tears are a sign of the re-integration of human being. It is nothing more than the fulfillment of the evangelical plan of Christ or the restoration of the Divine Image.[27]

But when the Holy Spirit fills the contemplative with His illumination through His fire of Divine Love, sorrow, joy and even tears cease as a predominant state. Man has entered into the Kingdom of Heaven that is within.

We find that in true mysticism, cultural differences seem to disappear and a common experience talks to all human beings who have had the courage and tenacity to enter into the "desert" of their heart and there do battle. The tears are a cry of imminent victory, that paradoxically fill the contemplative with sorrow and intense joy. The Jews of old who returned from their exile in Babylon wept profusely when they came home to their native land. They wept tears of sorrow to see the temple they loved, now destroyed. They wept tears of joy at realizing that Yahweh Lord had liberated them at last from their Babylonian captivity and now they were at "home."

Heaven is coming home to one's true self and tears herald the eternal celebration that we are risen in Christ Jesus, one with God, light from Light and this Light shall never be extinguished within us.

8

Night Vigil

One feature of the modern youth is its ability to break through a rather middle class concept of night as a time for sleep, day as a time for work. Today's youth thinks nothing of staying up all night, listening to music, leisurely enjoying each other's company, even at rare times on college campuses to cram through the entire night for the next day's exams. They see no great difficulty in sleeping in daytime if they have found themselves in a deep, intimate sharing mood the night before.

No doubt there is an "anonymous" form of eucharistic sharing and praying going on. But I wonder how many would pass even *one* hour in night prayer. How many Christians conceive prayer as work and therefore relegate it to daytime!

Still when we study early Christianity we see a universal habit among all Christians. They broke their sleep regularly and held a night vigil of prayer. They had developed this practice from the example of Jesus Himself. He went on the mountain top and spent many evenings absorbed in prayer before His Heavenly Father. "After saying good-bye to them, He went off into the hills to pray" (Mk. 6,46).

He exhorted His followers to be watchful! "So stay awake because you do not know when the master of the house is coming, evening, midnight, cockcrow, dawn; if he comes unexpectedly, he must not find you asleep. And what I say to you I say to all: Stay awake!" (Mk. 13:35-37).

St. John Chrysostom exhorts his 4th century Christians in commenting on Psalm 133: "Why does the Psalmist speak of praying in the night? He teaches us that the night is not to be completely spent in sleep and he shows that at night the prayers are purer, when also the mind is more uplifted and we are more at ease" (PG. 55,386).

This early Christian practice of interrupting one's sleep to keep a prayerful vigil contains an element of waiting for the Parousia. Even though St. Paul had to correct the mistaken ideas of the Thessalonians about the imminent return of Christ, there seems to be a deeper religious truth at stake here than the time-table of Jesus' second coming.

Praying at night after one has enjoyed several hours of deep, refreshing sleep, offers the Christian an experience of the Parousia as already here. Night is usually a time of indeterminateness; blackness ill-defines reality around us. We are thrown back into a primal fear of death and the unknown. Praying at night dispels such darkness and fear.

The light of Christ is experienced as truly overcoming the powers of darkness and sin, not only in one's soul but also in the world that is localized by the Christian's praying presence. This play on day and night, Christ and sin is well captured by St. Paul:

No, you are all sons of light and sons of the day; we do not belong to the night or to darkness, so we should not go on sleeping as everyone else does, but stay wide awake and sober. Night is the time for sleepers to sleep and drunkards to be drunk, but we belong to the day and we should be sober (1 Thess. 5:5-8).

Paradoxically Christians wait for His coming into their worlds and they discover that He does come. Although there is physical darkness all around and the spiritual sins of the day seem to litter the streets in grotesque ugliness, yet for the Christians who call out the coming of the Savior into this broken world, Jesus does come! He changes the night into day, darkness into light, sin into merciful, healing forgiveness. All because some Christians are calling upon Him at night to come!

They hasten His coming by letting Him come into the segment of their world as it is written in 2 Pet. 3:12,14: "...you should be living holy and saintly lives while you wait and long for the Day of God to come. . . .So then, my friends, while you are waiting, do your best to live lives without spot or stain so that He will find you at peace."

While the majority of people remain sleeping, a handful of Christians are waiting for the Bridegroom to come. In the middle of the night they cry out joyfully: "The bridegroom is here! Go out and meet him" (Matt. 25:6).

For one who has waited in the night for Jesus Christ to come, there is the Parousia experienced in his heart. Into the darkness and loneliness of his heart, Jesus comes as the first sliver of light breaking from the rising sun. Night is no more as the Word of God is born in his consciousness in a new enlightenment. How fitting a description of such nocturnal prayer we find in 2 Pet. 1:19: ". . .a lamp for lighting a way through the

dark until the dawn comes and the morning star rises in
your minds."

How often at 2 a.m. in my room in the Bronx,
overlooking the steamy, noisy, violent asphalt jungle of
New York, I have felt the coming of the Bridegroom. "A
lamp for lighting a way through the dark until the dawn
comes!" What a power the Christian of faith possesses as
he kneels in adoration before the Bridegroom! Much like
Mary the Mother of God, he brings forth Jesus, the Word
of God, and places Him again during the night into a cold,
bitter world that has no room for Him.

He stands with arms outstretched to greet the Savior
of the world on behalf of his fellow citizens. He intercedes
for the sick and the dying in hospital beds or in tiny,
stuffy tenement hovels that the Divine Healer would touch
their feverish brows and frightened, lonely souls and bring
them His loving strength.

Visions of young people crouched together in a
corner of Dionysian frenzy, high on drugs or alcohol, stir
him to compassion as he begs the Dawn to shine into their
minds, dispelling the darkness of such addiction. New
York is a real place. Just like night is real! Yet night is the
absence of dawn. And the Christian at night knows he has
the power through the Holy Spirit that prays within him
to hasten the Dawn of God's Word in the lives of those
humans living around him in darkness.

Charles DeFoucald beautifully describes his nightly
vigil:

Our Lord prays alone and prays at night. This His habit. . .Let
us love and cherish and practice this solitary nightly prayer of
which He sets us an example. It is very sweet to be alone in
intercourse with one one loves. With silence and peace and

darkness all-round. How sweet to speak alone with God at such times. . .Whilst everything sleeps, drowned in silence and darkness, I live at the feet of God, unfolding my soul to His love, telling Him that I love Him and He replying that I will never love Him, however great may be my love, as much as He cherishes me. . .Let me feel as I ought the value of such moments. Let me, following Your example, feel these hours of solitude and prayer by night to be more precious, more reposeful, more serene and more cherished than any others.

For those who have accustomed themselves habitually to such nightly vigils, it is a common experience that such deep, intimate prayer at the feet of Jesus Christ becomes a source of new-found repose and relaxation. I cannot offer strict scientific proof that one can obtain rest, not only through sleep, but also through sleep, prayer and more sleep in a way that one rises refreshed as though he enjoyed many more hours of sleep than the five or six he actually had. If one learns to open his psyche on a deep level to the healing, loving presence of the Divine Physician night after night, he soon experiences a strength and power of creativity during the day that makes him eager to share this with others. A "centering" endures throughout his busy day that fills him with peace and joy that no events can disturb or destroy. He pierces through the superficial opinions and values of the worldly-wise as though he were being directed into God's truth by an inner power.

Concentration on the task at hand becomes much easier since the source of so much distraction and diffusion of his mental powers, anxieties and a fear of loneliness, is dispelled by the enlivened consciousness of being situated in God's light. "You are all sons of light and sons of the day" (1 Thess. 5:5).

Much has to be de-mythologized about the desert Fathers. For most Christians it is impossible to flee from the world and live a life removed from the normal rhythms of most human beings. Yet every Christian is obligated to the evangelical work of being watchful and vigilant. If this is the essence of being a monk, then we must all become monks. Hesychius of Batos (7th century) defines the genuine Christian monk in these terms: "He alone is a true monk, in the real sense of the word, who practises interior vigilance and he alone is truly vigilant who is a monk in his heart."

The actual experience of being vigilant at night creates a psychosomatic vigilance that stays with the Christian throughout the day. An important part of the inward stillness necessary for Christians eager to pray on a deeper level, to pray the prayer of the heart comes from the quieting of all of man's psychic powers. Sleep does this naturally after about three or three and a half hours of deep sleep. Man is at his best prime time to meet God deeply within his "heart" if he takes his vigilant stance before His Creator in such a night vigil.

For a society that has allowed man to do anything else but pray during the night such a practice will immediately seem as though it were impractical and utterly insane. For monks far away from society and the pressures of urban living this can still be allowed. But for a modern Christian in our modern world!

It might just be worthy, however, of our experimentation with a new style of life as the early Christians did. They had experienced the Christ-event in their lives; they had read the Gospel story. The Parousia was taking place every day in their lives. They knew they had to be vigilant for He was coming! They were found like the five virgins with their lamps trimmed and they were awaiting His coming (Matt. 25:6-10). "And the ones who were ready went in to the wedding with him."

It just might be that the majority of Christians with their worldly wisdom will be found for most of their lives as the foolish five virgins, without oil in their lamps, who hear from the Bridegroom the terrifying words: "I tell you solemnly, I do not know you."

9

The Inward Call

Never before in human history has man been faced with a world of so much variety and exciting possibility to make him grow. Marshall McLuhan, the "oracle of the electric age," has characterized our age of instant information by its depth of involvement, decentralization, interdependence, instant speed, unified experience. With such instant communication available to us now, the world is becoming a "global village."

Yet modern technology has produced its own Frankenstein. It has produced its own demonic force that is blanketing the universe with a destructive power that propels itself toward a universal cataclysm at an alarming rate each day. The earth's deposit of natural resources are rapidly being consumed, leaving slag heaps in oceans of garbage. Fumes from man's machines rise up to cloud the atmosphere with a gaseous curtain that may throttle eventually any green life on planet earth.

Man stands frightened before such apocalyptic visions of a doomed planet earth. What happened to noble man that once danced joyously to soft music, thrilled to climb snow-capped mountains, loved to break bread with his friends and enjoy a cup of wine?

Carl G. Jung saw the need for man to know himself and the inner working of his psyche. He spoke in 1959 on a British Broadcasting telecast:

> One thing is sure—a great change of psychological attitude is imminent. That is certain. And why? Because we need more psychology. We need more understanding of human nature, because the only real danger that exists is man himself. He is the real danger, and we are pitifully unaware of it. We know nothing of man—far too little. His psyche should be studied, because we are the origin of all coming evil.

A universal *angst* or anxiety fills the heart of modern man with a sense of meaningless. His immersion in a pragmatic materialism has suffocated his communion with the Holy Spirit deeply within his innermost self. Thus cut off from an experienced relationship with God, the Absolute Transcendent, man is adrift on a dark, stormy ocean that threatens his very meaningfulness.

The Austrian psychiatrist, Viktor E. Frankl, explained man's plight in these terms:

> Effectively an ever-increasing number of our clients today suffer from a feeling of interior emptiness—which I have described as existential emptiness—a feeling of total absence of a meaning to existence. This is by no means a trait properly ascribable to the Western world only. Two Czechoslovak psychiatrists, Stanislav Kratochvil and Osvald Vymetal, have plainly drawn the attention in a series of articles to the fact that the lack of a meaning to life is a kind of "modern ailment," especially among younger people and that it is relentlessly encroaching upon capitalist and socialist institutions.[1]

Frankl gives two probable causes of this present existential emptiness to the forfeiture of the instinct and the loss of tradition. Man's instinct does not tell him, as animals' instinct does, what he *must* do. Because he has cut himself off from the roots of his past by throwing away traditions, he is at a loss as to what he *ought* to do. Usually he finds himself in the position that he does not know what he *wants* exactly. Conformism is the compromise for man of the Western hemisphere, while totalitarianism is the choice specifically common to the Eastern hemisphere. In a survey he conducted among students attending his course at the Vienna School of Medicine, 40% admitted experiencing a lack of significance to their own lives. But among his American students, it was 81%.[2]

And yet many in the West are eagerly seeking disciplines and techniques that will allow them admittance into an inner world of contact with the Transcendent. Either fed up with the gross materialism of their society or the loss of faith-community in their church affiliation, where they perhaps once had experienced God, they turn their attention to various forms of Far Eastern meditation. Too often such prayer is seen as a technique to help them therapeutically to "pull it all together" and not as worshipful praise and self-surrender to a Supreme God.

Still such interests in meditation techniques that teach man how to still his mind and enter into the deeper levels of his psyche can be an opening to deeper Christian prayer.

Charles Reich writes in the last chapter of *The Greening of America*: "Today we are witnesses to a great moment in history; a turn from the pessimism that has closed in on modern industrial society; the rebirth of a future; the rebirth of people in a sterile land."

The rebirth of modern society can only come about by a rebirth experienced in the deepest reaches of each individual. Unless man changes his interior world, his outside world will continue to reflect the disturbed world within him. Birth is the most fitting image to express the interior transformation of man's psyche powers so that he becomes a radiating force to build a community of love and peace and joy on this earth.

INNER SELF

One great temptation in today's world of gimmicks and practical do-it-yourself gadgets is that we can discover and awaken to ever-increasing intensity our *inner self* by some quick method. If we could only hit upon the right technique or find the suitable spiritual guide, we feel certain that this inner awakening would not only be facilitated but would surely reach its fullness.

But this is to forget that the inner self is not a compartment of our being. It is characterized primarily as a spontaneity and this necessitates our growth into greater personal freedom. Our inner self is a process of continued growth that involves our whole being. There we cannot start with a static concept and deduce its essential properties along with various infallible means of bringing it to fruition. This is to ignore the existential reality of our inner self.

It is man standing outside of his habitual fragmented self to experience himself as a *total* I, on his deepest and highest level of existence as a person. It is our life, lived fully with all our potential stretching forth with uncontained joy towards its spiritual fulfillment. Like a seed that has partially yielded to death, suddenly stretches forth to an unfolding inner power commanding greater life, so our inner life awakens to a new awareness of a more total and unified existence. When it is stirred, it communicates a new life to man's intelligence so that he reflectively and consciously lives on a deeper level. This awareness is not a thing we possess; it is a state of existence whereby we *are*. It is a real, indefinable experience of new living relationships of an *I* to God, to other human persons, to an energized world.

This experience of the inner self disappears or pales into a shadowy replica of reality under the scrutiny of rationalization. It cannot be put into a conceptualized "box." It is not a "thing" and hence there is no trick, no method, no "meditation" that can cajole it out of its hiding. A disciplined asceticism can only bring about the proper climate in which the inner self may both be recognized and be rendered more present. This climate produced by a spiritual regime includes such things as silence, poverty and detachment, purity of heart and indifference.

Still in every experience, whether religious, moral or artistic, that opens itself to the transcendent and spiritual world, there is some expansion of our inner self. Such a transcendent, spiritual experience takes on more and more beauty and meaningfulness accompanied by a certain incommunicability from the active participation of the inner self.

Here we can see how a certain spiritual and culturally transcendent atmosphere can favor the natural development of the inner self. Think of the peak of aesthetical beauty found in Eastern Byzantine Christianity that produced Liturgies as those of St. James, St. Basil, St.

John Chrysostom or the Medieval Gregorian chant or the stained-glass windows of Chartres. Such cultural values fostered a religious interior life. They nourished the development of the inner self according to all the phases of human growth, since they spoke in terms of basic, archetypal symbols and myths. Such a natural environment never made religious sentiment a self-conscious nervousness nor did it lead the individual into a gross subjectivity. Rarely do we meet with morbidity or extravaganza. Unfortunately, as Carl G. Jung has persistently pointed out, the West has become too cerebral and has lost the art of meeting the Transcendent Absolute through symbols and myths. A great need is felt to re-educate Westerners back to such a cultural setting that feels at home with the spiritual.

QUIET ZONE

True contemplation should not be taught, at least in the Christian vision of reality, as an extraordinary state reached by exceptionally gifted mystics. Contemplation is the state of living immanently in the depths of our being and there, through the infusion of God's Spirit of the gifts of faith, hope and love, to grow in ever-expanding consciousness that the Trinity abides there and dynamically energizes us by God's love.

It should be essential to every Christian to take Christ's words literally: "The kingdom of God comes unwatched by men's eyes; there will be no saying, 'See, it is here', or, 'See, it is there', The kingdom of God is here, within you" (Lk. 17:20-21; *Knox*). Every Christian should believe in the indwelling of God within him since Jesus Christ Himself had said: "If anyone loves Me, he will keep My word, and My Father will love him, and We shall come to him and make Our home with him" (Jn. 14:23).

This is the "good news" that should be a reality to all human beings. Most people are not aware of their great spiritual potential of living consciously a union with the Trinity. And yet this is what it means that God created man "according to His image and likeness" (Gen. 1:26). Great Christian mystics down through the centuries have always affirmed, as St. Symeon the New Theologian (+1022) and Meister Eckhart (+1327), that man's end is to contemplate the immanent God living within man and thus learn to adore and serve Him dwelling immanently throughout all of creation. As man becomes more aware of God's presence as not distant and extrinsic to man, he moves into a deep unity where his true self becomes a being in loving relationship to the indwelling God.

Rudolf Otto has well expressed Eckhart's mystical teaching:

He only has God for whom God is no longer objectum, who lives God, or rather "is lived by God," borne up and impelled by the Spirit and the power of God. But the more this is realized the more God as merely an object "disbecomes" from the sphere of his conceptions and thought, God becomes the inward power and the health of his spiritual life, so that the "living waters" in righteousness and holiness, love is radiated, and the spirit itself goes forth passing to others and working the same effects in them. He has got rid of the conceived and apprehended God, because God has now become his inward power, by which he lives, but upon which he reflects less, the more completely and powerfully he lives in the Divine.[3]

I have been calling this innermost part of our being, where we find the core of our true personality, the heart. Psychologist Carl Rogers calls it the "innermost self" where we get beyond preconditioning responses developed from our past life-experiences. Rogers, unlike Freud, insists that this core of personality is positive and healthy. In a statement backed up by twenty-five years of the practice . of psychotherapy, Rogers puts in a modern language a teaching confirmed universally by the early Greek Fathers in their optimistic view towards the "inner God-image" that can never be destroyed or marred by sin.

> One of the most revolutionary concepts to grow out of our clinical experience is the growing recognition that the innermost core of man's nature, the deepest layers of his personality, the base of his "animal nature," is positive in nature, is basically socialized, forward-moving, rational and realistic.[4]

It is, therefore, by plunging down into our innermost self that we make contact with God as healer. We are in direct contact with God as the vital source of our being. As long as we live superficially and dispersed amidst a world of ever-mounting multiplicity with an accompanying meaninglessness to all of it, we will not know the health of body, soul and spirit that God wishes us to enjoy.

In 1932 Carl Jung wrote a famous quote that has been repeated often since then. He said:

> During the past 30 years, people from all the civilized countries of the earth have consulted me...Among my patients in the second half of life—that is to say, over thirty-five—there has not been one whose problem in the last resort was not that of finding a religious outlook on life. It is safe to say that every one of them fell ill because he had lost

that which the living religions of every age have given to their followers, and none of them has been really healed who has not regained this religious outlook.[5]

THE CALL TO CONTEMPLATION

One enters into a state of contemplation almost imperceptibly. After years of disciplined prayer in which we were principally the main *doers*, pondering words and scenes from Holy Scripture, making comparisons, drawing conclusions, we realize gradually that we enjoy resting in the presence of God. He is within and I am aware of His personal loving activity in my regard. I learn to let go. I breathe psychologically more deeply, more peacefully. I am discovering that I can with ease go down into my inner self and stretch out joyfully with my spiritual hands that seek to grasp God who now is so close to me. I seem to be given new, interior eyes that lovingly gaze on Him. In that gaze I know myself in God's unique love for me. With new interior ears I ever so quietly listen to God as He communicates Himself to me without words, images or forms.

It is no longer my praying with this faculty or that, now thinking this thought, now that. My whole being is immersed in God. My disparate activities seem suspended as I enter into a tranquillity that brings to me a sense of oneness with God. Nikos Kazantzakis well describes the change from a discursive type of prayer to that of contemplation in his *Report to Greco*:

With the passage of days in this godly isolation, my heart grew calm. It seemed to fill with answers. I did not ask questions any more; I was certain. Everything—where we come from, where we are going, what our purpose is on earth—struck me as extremely sure and simple in this God-trodden isolation. Little by little my blood took on the godly rhythm. Matins, Divine Liturgy, Vespers, psalmodies, the sun rising in the morning and setting in the evening, the constellations suspended like chandeliers each night over the monastery; all came and went, came and went in obedience; I saw the world as a tree, a gigantic poplar, and myself as a green leaf clinging to a branch with my slender stalk. When God's wind blew, I hopped and danced, together with the entire tree.[6]

There is great peace in such periods of being immersed in the presence of God who resides at the center of my being. My prayer now is not something I do so much as entering into a state of being. *Enstasis*, a standing inside, best describes it. I seem to be standing inside my real self, standing not outside (*ecstasis*), but inside my deepest reality that brings with it a communion with God as my standing also *in* Him. I stand in His holy presence, loving Him without words or images. Yet the totality of my being is in a tranquil state of loving surrender.

St. John of the Cross well describes this psychological state:

> The surest sign is when the soul feels a need for remaining in solitude in amorous attention for God, without definite consideration, in interior peacefulness, quietude and tranquility, without exerting or exercising one's faculties. . .but only entertaining the said attentive mood and general amorous cognizance, without applying the intelligence to a particular aspect of God or even trying to understand Him.

One of the perplexing features of this deeper prayer of the heart is that the former ways that we used to measure our "praying ability" now seem no longer to apply. In fact, because one is less actively engaged with his imagination, understanding, will and affections, such can no longer be used as an index of our prayerfulness.

This is a state of expanded consciousness brought about by an increased infusion of faith, hope and charity by the Holy Spirit. It is only the Holy Spirit who assures us that we are united with God and truly growing in greater loving union. It is also the Holy Spirit who brings forth His gifts and fruit in our relationships toward others. Our lives, now rooted more deeply in the ultimate, reflect more exactly than at any other earlier stage the worth of our prayer-life.

PRAYING IN THE SPIRIT

The Holy Spirit dwelling within us teaches us how to pray deeply in the heart. ". . .the love of God has been poured into our hearts by the Holy Spirit which has been given us" (Rom. 5:5). It is God "who gives you His Holy Spirit" (1 Thes. 4:8). Our bodies through Jesus Christ have become temples of the Holy Spirit (1 Cor. 6:19). We are utterly incapable of praying to God as we should, but the Spirit prays within us.

> The Spirit too comes to help us in our weakness. For when we cannot choose words in order to pray properly, the Spirit Himself expresses our plea in a way that could never be put into words, and God who knows everything in our hearts knows perfectly well what He means and that the pleas of the saints expressed by the Spirit are according to the mind of God (Rom. 8:26-27).

It is the Spirit that gives life (Jn. 6:63). Jesus Christ's redemptive work takes place mostly in such deep prayer when He is releasing His Holy Spirit as He had promised He would (Lk. 11:13). The Spirit allows us to transcend beyond the limitations of our words and ideas about God in order to enter into the silent language of love as an experience that transcends anything human or controllable or wrought by our human powers. The Spirit of Jesus sent into our hearts allows us to know His presence and yield to His love towards the Father and the Son. ". . .you know Him because He is with you, He is in you" (Jn. 14:17).

What we experience continually when the Spirit prays within us is the utter conviction that we are God's beloved children. God loves us. But the good news that the Holy Spirit breathes forth within our hearts through an infused experience is that now we *know* that God loves us! We can cry out: "Abba, Father" (Rom. 8:15; Gal. 4:6).

> The proof that you are sons is that God has sent the Spirit of His Son into our hearts: the Spirit that cries, 'Abba, Father,' and it is this that makes you a son, you are not a slave any more; and if God has made you son, then He has made you heir (Gal. 4:6-7).

This Spirit "reaches the depths of everything, even the depths of God" (1 Cor. 2:10). It is thus that we are taught by God's very own Spirit of love, making us "spiritual" beings. If in deep prayer we are to touch the very depths of God, this can be done only through His Spirit. ". . .in the same way the depths of God can only be known by the Spirit of God. Now instead of the spirit of the world, we have received the Spirit that comes from God, to teach us to understand the gifts that He has given us. Therefore we teach. . .in the way that the Spirit teaches us; we teach spiritual things spiritually" (1 Cor. 2:11-13).

It is through the power of Jesus Christ's Spirit that our hidden selves are to grow strong, that Christ is to live in our hearts through faith. Through the Spirit we are able to grasp the breadth and length, the height and the depth of the love of Christ. The Spirit will fill us with the "utter fullness of God" (Ephes. 3:16-19).

Many persons interpret the phrase, "praying in the Spirit" to refer only to speaking in tongues, a gift of the Holy Spirit (1 Cor. 12:10). It admits of an infinitely larger experience of unending growth, both in this life and in the life to come. How can any human being comprehend the inexhaustible riches of the mind of God? And yet in the Spirit we do begin to contemplate the depths of the beauties and the love of the Father, Son and Holy Spirit. To contemplate is to move beyond our own activity to be activated by the power of the Holy Spirit. It means to be swept up into the Triadic love current of Father, Son and Holy Spirit. In the contemplative prayer of the heart, a gift of the Spirit praying within us, we move beyond feelings, emotions, even thoughts. The Spirit is so powerfully operative that we feel any activity of ours through imaging or reasoning can only be noise that disturbs the silent communication of God at the core of our being. One feels how images and words, man's own activity in prayer, now impose a restriction upon God who wishes to communi-cate Himself to us in a much more profound and total manner. If I start to speak words and fashion images of God and of ideas about Him, then I am limiting His freedom to speak His Word as He wishes, when He wishes. The Holy Spirit frees us so God can give Himself to us with utter freedom and joy.

TRANSFORMING PRAYER

Like Mary, the Mother of God, who opened herself in the Annunciation so totally to the Holy Spirit, as St. Luke records in his first chapter, we too allow that Word of God to be born within the depths of our being. Our "heart," the core of our being, becomes a womb that in silence and darkness receives God's Word. The Heavenly Father brings forth His Word within us, ever so gently, ever so gradually. Meister Eckhart was fond of speaking about this virginal birth of God's Word within man's deepest ground of being by the Heavenly Father.

> I have been asked what God is doing in heaven. I answer He has been giving His Son birth eternally, is giving birth now and will go on giving birth forever, the Father being in childbed in every virtuous soul. Blessed thrice is the man within whose soul the heavenly Father is thus brought to bed. All she surrenders to Him here she shall enjoy from Him in life eternal. God made the soul on purpose for her to bear His only-begotten Son. His ghostly birth in Mary was to God better pleasing than His nativity of her in flesh. When this birth happens nowadays in the good loving soul it gives God greater pleasure than His creation of the heavens and earth.[7]

The central teaching of Christianity is that God by grace is present in the soul of man, but how few people desire to live in the conscious awareness of this mystical union with God! Most of us are too immersed in sense knowledge and outgoing experiences. We lack the discipline and patience needed to cultivate the presence of God through the inward journey. Yet God is always ready through His Spirit who divinizes us by bringing us into the conscious awareness of our sonship with God, of our actual participation in His very own nature, as St. Peter insists on in 2 Pet. 1:4. The hindrance to a dynamic indwelling of God must be therefore ourselves.

To offset the hindrances that prevent this transforming presence of God's Spirit within us to be completely operative, we must be actively engaged in bringing our "passionate" nature under submission to the movements of the Spirit. Many Christians fear contemplation because they feel it leads them into quietism. True contemplation is hardly a sick, quietistic retreat into vacuity. It is for athletes who are ready with St. Paul to enter into the arena and do battle. Much diligent preparation is necessary if our spirit is to be brought into perfect accord with God's Spirit.

The Greek Fathers called this *praxis*, the active battle on our part to bring all of our irascible and concupiscible passions under the will of God. *Apatheia* is the Greek Fathers' word to describe a state of physical, psychical and spiritual silencing of all desires outwardly towards any object to possess it in self-love. It is a state of tranquillity or disinterestedness which is far removed from the evil of quietism that means having no interest in anything. The disciplined detachment taught by all spiritual directors in regard to higher contemplation is the removal of all self-centeredness in our desires and the placing of all our desires under the one dominating desire of God's directing will. This allows us then to desire the things of this world in the best possible way, according to God's measure and not our own egoistic manner of exploitation out of self-love.

RECOLLECTION

To move inwardly, we must learn to pull ourselves

toward our inner center. This is the work of the Holy
Spirit who brings all of the multiplicity of a long life of
learning and experience into a unity. Recollection in this
sense means more than recalling the presence of God from
time to time. In that English mystical classic of the 14th
century, *The Cloud of Unknowing*, the anonymous author,
relying heavily on Pseudo-Dionysius and his apophatic
approach to contemplation, teaches the necessity first of
the "cloud of forgetting" that allows the contemplative to
bring multiplicity, locked within his memory, into a
yielding only to God. It is a focusing upon God above all
else. A "blind stirring of Love," a gift from God's Spirit,
allows the contemplative to "let go and let God" reign
supreme in his life. Rigidity and prejudice in holding to
one's opinions and values are the two great enemies
hindering God's freedom from taking over in the contemplative's heart.

Love is the core and center of mysticism and God
begins to reveal Himself to the pilgrim that strips himself
from all attachments in order to be "recollected" or pulled
together into a "still point" of attentiveness in order that
God might speak. Then God reveals Himself in the
darkness of our own intellectual powers. Higher knowledge
of God cannot be achieved by any limiting conceptual
knowledge. Only an immediate, experimental knowledge
given by God when He wishes and to whomever He wishes
is the path to true contemplative knowledge. It is the
cloud of unknowing, the "docta ignorantia." It is the sole
work of God given ". . . .to the soul that He desires and this
without respect to the merit of the soul. Without this
grace, no saint or angel can conceive of seeking it."[8]

For moderns seeking to follow this call to deeper
contemplation, embracing this step, to live under the
"cloud of unknowing," is most difficult. Jacques Maritain

points out in his *Degrees of Knowledge* that approaching God in a manner that is beyond human concepts means that one must have conceptual knowledge beyond which he can go. The unwanted "ignorantia" is ignorance of what we do not know. The type of "unknowing" or ignorance in contemplation is the transcending of what we already know so that God can more directly reveal Himself without our prejudiced and limited, even erroneous, knowledge getting in the way of His communication.

Today there are many so-called "knowledgeable" persons formed in our universities. Much like computers, they store up in their brains mountains of facts. Unfortunately these facts are all too often unconnected, not pulled together into a coherent synthesis that can touch our lives and enrich them with operable knowledge. This may be one of the major factors why there are so few real contemplatives in our modern world of so much knowledge. Our conscious life is caught up so exclusively in intellectual abstractions, sense imagery, slogans and clichés from the political, social and economic world, all reinforced by a fierce sense of competition against the neighbor, that inner stillness in order to listen to God's deepest communications is almost impossible.

The state of breakthrough for the contemplative, caught between the "cloud of unknowing" or his inability of knowing God and the "cloud of forgetting" where he must forget created things, comes through the intense suffering caused by this sense of man's own helplessness and yet his suffering to possess God who is beyond him. Dr. Ira Progoff, commenting on this suffering state of the contemplative, explains the seeming separation.

> What is separating man from God is...the state of his consciousness. More specifically, it is man's consciousness of

his separateness, of his existence as an individual apart from God that keeps him separated from God.[9]

This "separateness" as a state of consciousness can be overcome by means of another psychological reality assumed by the individual. The gap of "separateness" can be bridged if the individual is able to render himself, with the grace of God, in a weakened psychological condition by yielding to his own conscious guidance of himself. "He must permit himself to drop into a condition of unconsciousness, a condition of total unknowing. This encompassing state of unconsciousness *is* the cloud of unknowing."[10]

The contemplative learns to let go by descending to the innermost ground of his being. Breaking through levels of consciousness, he sinks into the "cloud of unknowing," that state of unconsciousness within which the untapped regions beneath the surface of existence are revealed. Having reached this unconscious state devoid of all human thought and ideas, he is given the kind of knowledge of God that ordinary consciousness could not provide. The struggling and searching blindly in darkness are ended as he can now see "with a loving striving blindly beholding the naked being only of God Himself."[11]

DANGERS AND NEED OF DIRECTION

But in the struggling and searching within the deeper reaches of man's psyche, the contemplative encounters many difficulties. The reaching of the individual into the collective realm of consciousness must be an event which is prepared for and handled in an intelligent and mature way.

Throughout Carlos Castaneda's books Don Juan, the Indian Shaman, is constantly reminding Carlos, the disciple, that one must live like a warrior if he is to emerge in the desert victorious and not succumb to the power of the enemies that are all around him. One must be alert and trained to deal with the full existential realm of the interior life. If the individual is ill-prepared for the plunge into this deeper level of expanded consciousness, it will be totally self-destructive. Don Juan says: "The apprenticeship is long and arduous. . .in order to withstand the impact of such an encounter."[12] Kenneth Wapnick in an essay on mysticism and schizophrenia states: "The difference lies in the preparation."[13]

It is for this reason that every form of mysticism within a fixed religion has insisted strongly on a spiritual director, guru, shaman or roshi. The names differ but their roles are always the same. For the Christian mystic, in order that he can move progressively into greater conscious awareness of the indwelling Trinity and unlock the inner mysteries revealed by the awesome, transcendent God, he needs to be able to discern the authentic workings of the Holy Spirit from the evil spirits that so easily introduce "tares" where the Divine Sower sowed only good seed.

The spiritual father in the Christian tradition receives his title because he is a "spirit-filled" person, capable from his own experiences to traverse the circuitous ways of the interior life and from his knowledge of human nature and the study of Holy Scripture and theology to beget the disciple into the life of the Spirit. Perhaps the greatest function of the spiritual father is to warn the neophyte against the pitfalls of the inner world and to encourage him against the threat of what Paul Tillich calls *nonbeing*. Any of the states of expanded consciousness bring with them the anxiety of non-being. He writes in his book, *The Courage To Be*: "Basic anxiety is the anxiety of a finite being about the threat of non-being. ....Actualization of being implies the ability to take courageously upon oneself the anxiety of non-being."[14]

In such altered states of consciousness as witnessed in deep, contemplative prayer, alterations in thinking occur with the danger of subjective deviations in judgment, memory, attention and concentration. Often there can occur the sense of a loss of control and one's grip on reality. The sense of time and history is felt as well as emotional extremes vacillating between ecstasy and deep depression. These feelings can bring about intense sexual desires and movements. Voices can be heard very distinctly giving messages. Perceptual alterations including hallucinations, pseudo-hallucinations and increased visual imagery are perceived.

HOW TO HANDLE PSYCHIC PHENOMENA

God could certainly be speaking to the mystic through voices, visions and other psychic phenomena. Should we not accept these as gifts from God? Are they not a measure of one's spiritual growth? Not only the best spiritual guides on the mystical life within Christianity but also modern psychologists and psychiatrists point out that such phenomena can arise from within our psyche by a direct intervention from God; but also they can arise from the demonic forces within man, from man's own areas of repressed past experiences or from some diabolical forces outside of man working on his imagination.

What should be the firm advice received and followed

by one who is advancing in deeper contemplation is that which the great mystical doctor of the Church, St. John of the Cross, gives.

> And it must be known that although all these things may happen to the bodily senses in the way of God, we must never rely upon them or accept them, but we must fly from them, without trying to ascertain whether they be good or evil; for, the more completely exterior and corporeal they are, the less certainly they are of God. . .So he that esteems such things errs greatly and exposes himself to great peril of being deceived; in any case he will have within himself a complete impediment to the attainment of spirituality.[15]

Too often, especially among charismatic Christians who begin to experience a deeper hunger for contemplation and silent prayer, the phenomenon of seeing intellectual visions or hearing clear voices or smelling heavenly odors or receiving delicate touches from supernal beings can be very easily (and erroneously) often interpreted as a sign of God's predilection and a growth in deeper prayer. St. Teresa of Avila fell into this error in the early part of her spiritual life. It is almost impossible to have a "perfect" mystical experience with vivid impressions upon our senses and interior faculties that is solely from God. There can be so much of our own repressed areas of experiences projecting themselves upon the reality of our consciousness to lead us to believe that what we are experiencing is true reality. Therefore it is almost impossible for a contemplative or one's spiritual director to discern whether a given psychic experience is solely from God or it contains a mingling of self-projection with a dash of demonic interference.

The important point that must be made here is that for those who are eager to progress in true, mystical prayer, the way to complete union with God is through pure faith without the aid of anything we can know either naturally or supernaturally. I do not mean to say that God cannot be gifting the contemplative with real graces that can be of a strong supportive nature. Any real growth in prayer usually brings with it at some time or other some movement towards a "well-being" with God that can admit of various degrees of intensity and repercussions in our sense and psychic life. But in the words of counsel of the great mystic, St. Bernard of Clairvaux, we are to seek, not the experience of God, but the God of experience.

The great danger in mystical experiences is that they can be so alluring to us. We are lifted outside of ourselves. A sense of power and new regeneration comes over us and it is most difficult not to want this experience over and over again. Especially when we have been brought up reading the lives of the Saints, it becomes a natural conclusion that because such Saints experienced similar experiences, then we are fast approaching the mansion where the halos are distributed! By not only ignoring such experiences when they come but by also not wanting in any way such to happen, one cuts out any self-inordination. If such come to us as gifts from God, they will surely bring to us what God intended by giving them. We will be greatly strengthened and still we will remain detached from them.

Again St. John of the Cross gives us a solid bit of advice:

> If such experience be of God, it produces its effect upon the spirit at the very moment when it appears or is felt, without giving the soul time or opportunity to deliberate whether it

will accept or reject it. For, even as God gives these things supernaturally, without effort on the part of the soul, and independent of its capacity, God produces in it the effect that He desires by means of such things;. . .it is as if fire were applied to a person's naked body: it would matter little whether or not he wished to be burned; the fire would of necessity accomplish its work.[16]

Thus we see that contemplatives are never to desire such communications or experiences from God. They must not seek to retain them if they do occur but, like pilgrims, they must push on, trusting that whatever good effect the Lord intended will remain.

UNION OF WILLS

The "new" knowledge that God gives of Himself to the purified contemplative is an experience of God's ardent, personalized love for the contemplative. Such an experienced love calls out a return of love. But love cannot be merely spoken in words. For the contemplative who has deeply experienced God's love by being begotten through Jesus Christ in His Holy Spirit in the deepest recesses of his being, the reaction is a way of life that is characterized by the merging of man's will with the will of God. Man can measure the degree of God-love he has experienced in contemplation by measuring the degree of surrendering to the will of God. When God's will and man's will are in union, then God can act, live and create through that person.

Then the Holy Spirit in an analogous way, as He unites the will of the Father to the Son and the Son to the

Father in mutual, loving surrender, so He effects within man's heart a similar union of wills. Then the contemplative can understand what it means to pray in the Spirit. It is God's Spirit within man that is praying, not by words, but by a movement of surrendering love that seeks always to please the Beloved in all things.

The Holy Spirit grasps the contemplative in the totality of his being. It is a true "ecstasis" now, standing outside of his habitual way of thinking and acting. It is an ecstasy, not of enthusiasm that passes when the "warm" glow disappears before the harsh realities of a world that is groaning in travail (Rom. 8:22), but an ecstasy of adoration of God dwelling within the heart of the contemplative. It is an ecstasy of self-surrendering service to the majesty of God. Having God within as the vital force of the contemplative, he knows by an ever-growing experience that He is touching the intimate bond of all creation. In his loving relationship to God, the contemplative is impelled with the total openness of his being outwardly into the community nearest him to find God there as the creative force.

Such a contemplative, who lives deeply, touching always in an expanding consciousness the innermost core of his being and there discovering the loving presence of God, is convinced that true love for God will bring forth the strongest love for others. Indeed, he begins to feel the tremendous uncreated energies of the loving Trinity within and he yields himself to their movement. This movement is always one "towards," an emptying motion towards a receptacle to receive its offering of unselfish love.

In such interior prayer where words and affections, images and intellectual acts no longer serve as a measure of our union with God in prayer, we must now rely exclusively on our living relationships towards others to measure whether we have been truly touching the God of love and have been transformed into new creatures by His ardent love. Any authentic contemplative prayer must be measured not by psychological phenomena that may occur during prayer, such as visions, voices, levitation, inner warmth, but ultimately by the love and humility we show towards those around us. "Let us love one another. For love is of God and everyone that loves is born of God and knows God" (1 Jn. 4:7). It is toward our neighbor therefore that the prayer of the heart now turns us.

10

Finding God in the Human

Throughout all of Christianity the truth that Jesus Christ came to reveal to us by means of His own incarnation has undergone every conceivable attack by heresies that refused to live in the paradoxical language of mystery. That God should so love us as to give us His only begotten Son (Jn. 3:16) seems utterly preposterous in the light of the claims of all other religions. How could God, especially the Jews asked, who is so immaterial, take on matter? How could the Eternal step into time and begin to exist? How could the invisible suddenly be rendered visible before our human eyes? How could the Giver of life receive life and be born of a woman?

If Jesus Christ's divinity has been denied throughout 20 centuries of Christianity, it is also understandable that similar objections would have been raised against His humanity. The Docetists, against whom St. Paul and St. John in the 1st century were fighting, insisted that Jesus Christ could not have taken on Himself a full, material, human nature. Matter was evil and utterly incapable of "revealing" God to a sinful world locked in matter as in a prison. The Monophysites wanted His humanity to be somehow swallowed up, leaving only a divine nature and person. The Apollonarians, against whom the Cappadocians, Basil, Gregory of Nazianzus and Gregory of Nyssa, waged a written campaign for a true Christology, held that in Jesus' human nature there was no full human soul, otherwise He would have been able to have sinned.

So throughout the long history of Christianity there has been the precarious struggle to bring together the godly and the human, divinity and corporeality in Jesus Christ so that each element of each nature, divinity and humanity, was completely intact, without division or confusion, as the Chalcedonian Christology stated it.

There seems to be a hidden presupposition in the extreme positions about the union of the two natures of Jesus Christ, namely, if He is considered to be a most human being, then He cannot quite be also God. If He is divine, then the humanity in Him has to be somehow made defective or be swallowed up into non-existence. True Christianity grew out of the experiences of the Apostles and followers of Jesus Christ as recorded in the New Testament. St. John the Evangelist insists that he had seen and touched this man, Jesus Christ (Jn. 20:30-31; 1 Jn. 1:1). "This disciple (St. John) is the one who vouches for these things and has written them down, and we know that his testimony is true" (Jn. 21:24).

HUMANITY REVEALS DIVINITY

St. John is the "beloved disciple" of Jesus. He had experienced deeply the unique love of Jesus for him as a person. We can imagine that Jesus was not afraid to love others humanly and uniquely, if He allowed John to recline on His breast at the Last Supper in full view of the other Apostles. St. John's Gospel records other human encounters with others like Nicodemus, the Samaritan adulteress, those at the wedding feast at Cana, the man born blind, Lazarus, Mary and Martha, Judas at the Last Supper, Thomas the Doubter, Peter repentant. Always Jesus is totally human, completely "with" the situation.

We might say that His divinity shines through His perfect human relationships. One is not sacrificed for the other, but, on the contrary, for St. John and the other early disciples, it was apparently precisely by being fully human that Jesus manifests His divinity. And by being fully divine, the Logos from all eternity, Jesus Christ, can perfectly manifest to the human world what *real man* should be like.

From the pages of the Gospel accounts we find Jesus Christ meeting each day's events with a marvelous freedom of heart. He shows a complete at-homeness with the human situation. He relishes eating at the banquet table of Simon the leper or sharing a cup of cold water with the adulterous Samaritan woman at the well of Jacob. "The Son of man comes eating and drinking." He evidently loved other human beings. Women loved Him and He manifested His love towards them. Mary, the sister of Lazarus, lovingly washed His feet and anointed them, sat at His feet and lovingly touched them and Jesus was completely at home enjoying it all, even praising Mary for her attention to Him. He rejoiced with God's creation in all of nature as we see from His constant references to creatures that He evidently had experienced in joyful encounters as a child. The whole world was charged with His Father's presence and He knew all was created good.

A BEYONDNESS

Still there permeates throughout His life a strength that allows Him to be above each situation, each human encounter, each material creature enjoyed. He preserved a certain distance from it all. The world was distinct, profane from Him and His Father. It was not the end of His love. He stood infinitely beyond all creatures. Something in Him was not engaged in the human development. Or better, we could say that in each human encounter Jesus was leading each person beyond the human to a self-revelation of His divinity.

How clearly this is seen in His conversation with the Samaritan woman at the well of Jacob. He was totally interested in her and that total human giving meant that He wanted her to accept Him as the Christ. He leads her to thirst for the living water that He promises to give her. He cannot be side-tracked by her entering into religious polemics of where one is to worship God. He uses everything in this conversation to go beyond into the realm of truth — that He is the Messiah and the Father now wants true worshippers who will worship in spirit and truth (Jn. 4:23).

The essence of Jesus Christ's incarnation consists in His total divinity imaging the infinite love of the Heavenly Father through His humanity. As we experience His great human love for us, especially on the Cross, we are led to His divinity. Because He is so fully human, we can more readily be led into a relationship with the Godhead.

FROM MAN TO GOD

What we experience by encountering the same loving

Jesus in His full humanness in the pages of the New
Testament, we also experience in our human relationships
with one another. Although we are not, as Jesus Christ,
divine by nature, by living lives that are fully human and
open to a greater sharing in transcending beauty, we
manifest the divine both to ourselves and to others that we
truly love.

To be moving towards deeper, human relationships
means to be revealing more of God's loveliness to others in
our relationships. This is not, according to our Christian
faith, a mere extrinsicism that means we resemble somewhat what God would be like in human form. Our faith
convinces us that it is actually God's very own life
dynamically living in us and revealing His divinely loving
presence within us outwardly toward others.

FROM GOD TO MAN

The prayer of the heart brings us into a deep healing
of our loneliness and basic isolation that sinful self-
centeredness develops and fosters. God's loving presence
calls us into a share of the triadic community that dispels
fear, anxieties, hatred and unforgiveness. Walls that we
have built up to secure what we thought was our true
identity and dignity before a hostile world now come
shattering down.

Experiencing God's love deeply gives us a new-
founded sense of our true self. Deep prayer has allowed
the potential within us toward divinized children of God
to burgeon forth into actualization. We know the abiding
power of God, loving within us. "If we love one another,
God dwells in us and His love is perfected in us. . .and we

have known and believed the love that God has for us. God is love; and he that dwells in love dwells in God and God in him" (1 Jn. 4:12,16). It is a new power, the love of Christ, that has gained mastery in our lives (2 Cor. 5:14-15). No longer do we operate according to our own value-structures, under our own independent power, but it is now the love-energy of Jesus Christ that lives and loves in us (Gal. 2:20).

Prayer of the heart, whether experienced by a hesychastic father in a cell on Mount Athos of the 14th century or by a housewife in downtown Chicago, universally effects the same experience. The closer man touches God in his heart, the closer is he also drawn to a union of love towards his neighbor.

St. Dorotheus of the 6th century used the example of a wheel. The closer the spokes of the wheel moved to the center, the closer they came to each other. The farther they moved out from center, the more distance separated one spoke from another. It was Evagrius in the Egyptian desert of the 4th century who declared that "I leave men in order to find them."

ONENESS WITH THE WORLD

In deep, interior prayer the love that thus emerges is not forced or contrived, although it is not easily achieved; one becomes aware of a deeper self emerging and surrenders the will in sacrifice and penitential practices in order that this true self might come to fullest development in God and consequently one finds himself in true communion with both God and neighbor.

Thomas Merton well describes this universal sense of "oneness" with all men through silent immersion in God:

. . .it is in fact the function of solitude to make one realize such things with a clarity that would be impossible to anyone completely immersed in the other cares, the other illusions, and all the automatisms of a tightly collective existence. . .It is because I am one with them that I owe it to them to be alone, and when I am alone they are not "they" but my own self. There are no strangers![1]

The deeply prayerful Christian who has learned to dwell within his heart is very much a part of his contemporary world without at the same time becoming "worldly." If God has created this world good, the contemplative, who has purified his heart and begins to see God everywhere in His beautiful creation, wants to bring forth God's creative power that calls him out to be a cooperator, "a reconciler" as St. Paul frequently calls man, the new creature in Christ Jesus (2 Cor. 5:17-18).

Again Thomas Merton summarizes the contemplative's relationship with the world:

The world as pure object is something that is not there. It is not a reality outside us for which we exist. . .the world has in fact no terms of its own. . .we and our world interpenetrate . . .If anything, the world exists for us, and we exist for ourselves. It is only in assuming full responsibility for our world, for our lives and for ourselves that we can be said to live really for God.[2]

CONCERN FOR THE POOR

The early Fathers realized that the heart of Christianity focused on a deep concern toward the poor, the suffering, the afflicted. They had experienced the compas-

sionate mercy of the Heavenly Father through the incarnate Jesus Christ and this divine love drove them to
become incarnate compassion towards all the poor around
them. But they knew poverty could admit of many levels;
the most evident was that of physical poverty: persons
starving from want of food and drink, the naked and
homeless, the sick and dying with all of their needs.

The great mystics of Eastern Christianity have been
accused of being too much immanently present to God
indwelling them and not enough of being toward the
transcendent God in others on a horizontal plane of
self-giving to others. Yet these early Fathers had long
meditated on the Gospel. They knew the teaching of the
Master:

> For I was hungry and you gave Me food; I was thirsty and you
> gave Me drink; I was a stranger and you made Me welcome;
> naked and you clothed Me, sick and you visited Me, in prison
> and you came to see Me. Then the virtuous will say to Him in
> reply, 'Lord, when did we see You hungry and feed You; or
> thirsty and give You drink? When did we see You a stranger
> and make You welcome; naked and clothe You; sick or in
> prison and go to see You?' And the King will answer, 'I tell
> you solemnly, insofar as you did this to one of the least of
> these brothers of Mine, you did it to Me.' (Matt. 25:35-40).

They knew faith without good works was dead. St.
James had clearly taught them this basic Christian attitude
towards the poor: "If one of the brothers or one of the
sisters is in need of clothes and has not enough food to live
on, and one of you says to them, 'I wish you well; keep
yourself warm and eat plenty,' without giving them these
bare necessities of life, then what good is that? Faith is like

that: if good works do not go with it, it is quite dead" (James 2:15-17).

It was St. Basil who had lived the prayer of the heart so deeply that he set up the first Christian hospitals and orphanages to take care of the sick and the fatherless. In Greece today "basilios" is still the name given to hospitals, named after St. Basil, the contemplative, who knew that it was the love of Christ that urged him to be kind to the poor.

Such holy Fathers call us back to a basic Christian view that can only be accepted and understood by persons who pray. In today's society more stress is placed on the private ownership of property and wealth, but in the 4th and 5th century of these spiritual giants of God, they taught that material possessions were essentially common property belonging to all mankind. Their deep prayer made them realize the "koinonia," the community of all mankind under one loving Heavenly Father. God had bequeathed His creation and all creatures, not to a few individuals, but to mankind. St. Basil speaks of a "common and universal sharing of possessions. It is lawful for each one to take from these common possessions to the degree that he is able and that is suited to his needs."[3]

In those early centuries of Christianity this was the common teaching also among the Western Fathers. St. Ambrose boldly claims that the distinction between rich and poor is not according to nature. The cause of our social inequalities is therefore not some God-given law natural to mankind but it is something introduced into human society through man's selfishness. Poverty for such mystical Fathers is not something inevitable and to be expected. They believed and hoped that it could disappear as men learned to pray and be enlightened to see God's

order of creation. This is the common teaching of the
Fathers as voiced by St. Ambrose:

> The Lord our God willed that this earth should be the
> common property of all mankind and so, He offered its
> produce for all to enjoy; but man's avarice distributed the
> right to its possession.[4]

Deep prayer of the heart allowed such contemplatives
of the early Church to realize keenly the need of sharing
riches with all. All men had a strict right to the use of what
they needed to live decently. Those who possess more of
talents and of wealth of this earth have a need to share
these with the poor. They are merely God's administrators
of a common possession given them by God to be
distributed to all in need. One cannot justify possessing
great wealth by appealing to a poverty of detachment that
lies only in the "spirit" and never quite condescends to
become a true detachment in act of actual sharing the
wealth with the needy. Again, we see from these great
contemplatives that this sharing of one's wealth with the
poor is not a generous condescension on the part of the
wealthy but it flows from the spiritual insight that the
poor have a right in justice to receive a share of wealth that
must be common to all since it rightfully belongs to God,
the Father of all.

The ancient apostolic writing, *The Didache*, put it
succinctly:

> Do not turn away from the needy; rather, share everything
> with your brother, and do not say, 'It is private property.' If
> you are sharers in what is incorruptible, how much more so in
> things that perish.[5]

St. Ambrose describes the alms that the rich give to the poor as being a real restitution, something that is due to the poor man in strict justice. "It is not from your own possession that you are bestowing alms on the poor; you are but restoring to him what is his by rights. For, what was given to everyone for the use of all, you have taken for your exclusive use. The earth belongs not to the rich, but to everyone...Thus, far from giving lavishly, you are but paying part of your debt."[6]

COMMON CHRISTIAN DOCTRINE

Such a Christian attitude towards the poor cannot be attributed to an exaggerated, oratorical language of preaching bishops of the early Church. It is the common doctrine taught by all teachers of the Christian life in the first five centuries, both in the East and West. Even in recent times in Christian Russia before the Revolution, when the State was not overly concerned with helping the sick and the poor, each Christian, as he left the Sunday Liturgy, walked down the line of beggars and the sick and placed as much of his money into their outstretched hands as he could afford. The children also were instructed to give something to each poor person. More importantly, they were taught never to wait for the beggar to thank them for their kindness, but rather they were to bow before the beggar and thank him that he allowed them to find Christ in him by sharing whatever was superfluous to them.

St. Basil gives us a famous passage that well summarizes this involvement with the poor:

The bread that you hold back belongs to the hungry; the coat that you hoard in your cupboard belongs to the naked. The shoe that is gathering mildew in your home belongs to the unshod; the money you have hoarded belongs to the poverty-stricken. Thus, you are oppressing as many people as you could have helped with your possessions.[7]

If, as the Fathers claim, wealth has no other purpose than that of being shared, it follows that the rich will become less rich and they will simply cease to be rich. But they were drawing their conclusions from their prayer over Holy Scripture.

A CONCERNED CHRISTIAN

Today any serious Christian who prays deeply in the heart is impelled to be concerned with the rampant poverty throughout the world. He cannot muffle his ears and block out the cries of his suffering brothers and sisters wherever in the world they may be the victims of oppression, wars or natural calamities.

Some Christians lose their credibility before the world by claiming that in their prayer they have encountered a loving, compassionate God while before a hungry world they continue to be well-fed and callously unconcerned with the poor and needy. Before the Church, which is you and I, in our concrete world can lift its voice to alleviate the suffering, it must first in you and me allow that anguish cry for justice to find an echo in our hearts.

Too long has the Church along with its "religious" people been too caught up in a Platonic dualism that pits God's world of the spirit against the world of matter. A "prayerful" person in such thinking could easily enough, in the trenchant words of Diedrich Bonhoeffer, kick his heels before such "mundane" concerns and fly off to an "other-worldly" region where all was harmoniously beautiful. The only difficulty was that it was not God's world. And God is to be incarnated in a material world!

AN INVOLVED CONCERN

If our prayer of the heart is to be authentic and deeply transforming, we will measure its success by the loving concern we have toward others, especially those who have the greatest need, physically, psychically and spiritually. A hermit adoring God in his heart may not be able to do much to bring food or clothing to the needy if he is completely removed by his specialized, eschatological vocation of interceding day and night for the needs of all mankind. However, his prayer must open himself to the needs of all men, even though he meets them on a more spiritual level.

For others of us, each according to our state of life and opportunities, we are called to be completely open to share ourselves in order to bring others into a greater opportunity to grow as human beings in a manner befitting children of God.

Pope Paul VI in his Apostolic Exhortation, *Evangelica Testificatio*, addressed to Catholic religious in matters of poverty, violence and justice, answers his question as to how the cry of the poor will find an echo in the lives of seriously dedicated Christians: "That cry must, first of all, bar you from whatever would be a compromise with any form of social injustice."[8]

The man of prayer seeks to live the Gospel. But the

Gospel is not primarily a blueprint for overcoming social injustices to bring about a world of equality for all. Yet it does enter the political, social and economic arenas as a prophetic witness to God's promises of justice, peace and universal brotherhood. Here we can see the Church, as the magisterium or teaching body, has an obligation to be in the mainstream of the contemporary world, recalling to world leaders the Gospel principles.

YOU ARE THE CHURCH

Still the Church is you and I and all who wish to live in Jesus Christ. As there are many cells and organs in the human body, St. Paul reminds us, so there are many members in the Body of Christ, the Church. A Cesar Chavez, a Dorothy Day and a Helder Camara will witness as prophets of the Gospel differently from a Christian policeman, nurse, monk or housewife.

But the important element in true, authentic prayer is that all of us will constantly be thrust forth into our immediate communities and there witness to the Gospel values by fighting all social injustices, according to our talents and charisms.

The Gospel account of Jesus praying for 40 days in the desert and then being tempted before He went out into His community of Palestine to preach the Kingdom of God can serve us as an analogy of our own prayer-life and our social concern. It would be beyond the scope of this book to detail a theology of liberation and social reform. But it is necessary to see that our prayer moves us in action to serve God's created world.

TEMPTATIONS IN THE DESERT

Jesus is tempted by Satan to turn stones into bread. Yet he does multiply two loaves to feed thousands. The great temptation that all persons of prayer must combat is the urge to possess inordinately the things of the earth. We must then fight against any principle of monopolizing that would create injustice in the social order.

Man is constantly tempted to be recognized as superior to others and hence is plagued with status symbols and an incentration that destroys a movement towards a community in loving service. Jesus thwarts the temptation in the desert by refusing to hurl himself from the Temple in order to impress the crowds. Yet He humbly serves to multiply healings and miracles to help the suffering.

Nietzsche believed it was the "will to power" that pushed man to attain new heights of excellence. Yet Jesus refuses to have power over the kingdoms of the world. Instead, He comes as the suffering Servant, washing the feet of His brothers and teaching them that true power is to learn of Him who is meek and humble of heart.

Prayer leads one into an inner conversion by which man can have God's truthful attitude towards other men and the creatures of this world. But true prayer also leads man to effect a similar conversion or liberation in the world around him. Such a prayerful Christian will seek according to his circumstances to bring about an economic order that will provide the starving poor throughout the world with a more equitable distribution of God's wealth to mankind. He will struggle that in the social order new structures will allow each man to evolve according to his

God-given dignity as a free thinking and loving individual and a responsible member of his society. The man of the heart will be concerned that in the political arena power will not be monopolized and exercized by a few but that the whole *polis* and its leaders exist to serve the community and all the individuals who form that community.

SPIRITUAL CONCERN

A person of deep prayer partakes of the infinite compassion and love of God who gradually by His Holy Spirit effects a divinizing process in him. He does not distinguish between this or that need, bodily, psychical or spiritual. His self-giving simply goes out toward a total individual. It is this or that needy person whom he seeks lovingly to serve.

His horizontal relations, therefore, towards others are not merely limited to their extrinsic needs. The many psychic and spiritual needs of all who present themselves to the person of deep prayer are also his concern. Being sensitive in prayer to the goodness of God toward himself, he, more than most humans who do not pray habitually, wants others to share the love, peace and joy that he has abundantly experienced from God's loving hands in prayer. The more God becomes a living reality to his consciousness, the more he wants to share this reality with others. St. Paul grasped the role of reconciling others to God once he was so reconciled. "And all things are of God who has reconciled us to Himself by Jesus Christ and has given to us the ministry of reconciliation" (2 Cor. 5:18).

St. Paul wanted to become all things to all men in order to win them for Christ. "I made myself a Jew to the

Jews, to win the Jews. . .For the weak I made myself weak. I made myself all things to all men in order to save some at any cost; and I still do this, for the sake of the Gospel, to have a share in its blessings" (1 Cor. 9:20-22).

Such a Christian, realizing what an eternity without the knowledge and love of Jesus Christ would be like, spends himself to share the riches of faith that he has received. His time is at the service of others; he is the servant mediating the healing love of Jesus Christ to all who knock on his door. All of his physical, psychical and spiritual talents are ready to be used to help others know the love of God. And when time and circumstances do not permit more direct sharing in loving service, such a person of prayer stretches out his arms in intercessory prayer.

St. Symeon the New Theologian expresses such loving service through prayerful intercession for his neighbor:

> . . .he would wish with such zeal the salvation of his brothers, that often he would beg God, the Lover of men, with all his soul, with burning tears either to save them with him or to condemn him with them, refusing absolutely to be saved alone and in this imitating the attitude of God and that of Moses. So greatly tied spiritually to them by holy charity in the Holy Spirit, he would not even wish to enter into the Kingdom of Heaven if he had to be separated from them.

TO BE IS TO LOVE

We exist in order to be loved and to love. The more we receive of God's love, the more we can give love to others. Albert Camus' *The Fall* is a contemporary psychological description of what happens when a human being refuses to "become involved" by a loving service toward others who need our love. Man creates his own hellish condition.

But true love towards our neighbor is an accurate thermometer of the degree of love of God that lives within us. God is love, says St. John over and over again. He is outpouring love. We exist sheerly because God is He-who-always-gives-Himself. We are empty receptacles of God's goodness, said St. Irenaeus in the 2nd century. When in deep prayer we experience God's love for us as an habitual giving of Himself to us, we then, by the power of the uncreated energies of God loving us, are given the power to do what we could not do on our own. We can love all who come to us. It is always God's love in us that empowerizes us. And even though we fail to love as we ought, God reveals Himself as healing love within us. It is in our seeking to love our neighbor that God makes it possible. And the more we desire to love all men, the more God's love will be perfected in us.

The Christian who prays in the heart understands from experience the beautiful words of St. John, the "beloved disciple:"

> My dear people,
> let us love one another
> since love comes from God
> and everyone who loves is begotten by God and knows God.
> Anyone who fails to love can never have known God,
> because God is love. . .
> My dear people,
> since God has loved us so much,
> we too should love one another.
> No one has ever seen God;
> but as long as we love one another
> God will live in us
> and His love will be complete in us (1 Jn. 4:7-12).

11

Heaven: Interacting Love

Dr. Harold Urey, one of the inventors of the atom bomb, wrote shortly after one of the early atomic explosions on the desert flats of New Mexico: "I am trying to frighten you. I am myself a frightened man. All the experts I know are also frightened." It is reported that these experts waited for this explosion with faces to the ground. Even the most unbelieving of them felt something like a prayer rising in their hearts. It was like a prayer of a young knight on the eve of his consecration. At that historic moment mankind ended its adolescence. Man entered into his new role as master of the created world.

Man of the 20th century, so powerful with all his newly discovered science, yet cringes in the corner of this universe afraid, feeling the need of Someone beyond himself; Someone even more powerful than man; above all, Someone who, unlike man, is totally and consistently unselfish; Someone who is Love itself.

We are not surprised that a static, scholastic theology which had placed the casualities of God and man into neatly arranged boxes would give way to a process theology in the exploding 20th century that then would lead to a theology of hope. Another approach would be to see through the steady growth in personalism, accentuated by a dehumanizing, anonymous cosmopolitan society of masses and statistics, a greater understanding in our own unique identity achieved through more meaningful, more consciously loving relations with others around us.

I would maintain, without claiming any "astralgic" powers, that theology will soon see a full-bloom preoccupation, steming from a theology of hope and personalism, with the problem of Heaven, Purgatory and eschatology. But this study will have nothing in common with the short theses tucked into manuals of scholastic theology that usually dealt with the four last things: death, Heaven, Hell and Purgatory. The main reason for such a new approach to these teleological problems is that process theology is breaking through the dichotomies that have presented death as a punishment, heaven as a reward and hell as an eternal damnation. The inter-related dichotomies that have shaped our distorted views of what happens to us when we die, and hence that have grossly created a caricature of God, are those that posited as truly existing, separated, distinct and unrelated concepts as body and soul, matter and spirit, nature and supernature, life and death, Heaven and Hell.

PROCESS PHILOSOPHY

Names such as Alfred North Whitehead, Henri Bergson, Charles Hartshorne, Daniel Day Williams, Norman Pittenger and Schubert Ogden stand in the forefront of process thinkers associated with a philosophic-theological focus on an evolutionary view of the world both in process of evolving and as a process. In such thinking the world is dynamic rather than a static reality. Human nature is no longer described as an immutable and unchanging thing. Man is an open-ended "society" or "organism," living, changing, developing, acting on and being acted upon by an endless number of relationships.

Therefore the world and all that is in it is an interrelated society of "occasions." There is no possibility of isolating one occasion from another so that each may be considered in itself alone. Into each given occasion there enters past events as well as present pressures and always there is the "lure" of the future. Thus you and I are incapable of existing in complete isolation from other humans or from our own past history or from any of the developments of mankind in general. In being "yourself" you are all that has gone on within you and around you. Norman Pittenger writes, "We live in and we are confronted by a richly interconnected, interrelated, interpenetrative series of events, just as we ourselves are such a series of events."[1]

What in a scholastic philosophy was seen as a chain of cause and effect is seen in this process system in a much richer understanding of occasions, pressures, movements and events which come to focus at this or that point. There is a rejection of the dualism which make divisions between mind and matter, natural and supernatural. God's relationships towards our created world and ourselves involve a concrete process. God shares with His creatures a degree of freedom so that God's interaction with His creatures involves real intercommunication. What happens in the world is of *real* concern to God.

PROCESS THEOLOGY IN THE GREEK FATHERS

When we read the Greek Fathers, especially St. Basil, St. Gregory of Nyssa, St. Maximus the Confessor and St. Gregory Palamas, we are presented with a very similar process theology, one that was articulated by these Fathers out of their mystical prayer-life that had its roots in Holy Scripture. Rather than an antithesis between nature and supernature, they opposed natural and unnatural. Nature was not only the embryonic seed but the fulfillment in all the creature's final fruition. Man's nature was always destined, not only by God's finality in creating man, but also in God's loving activity to accomplish His plan, to make man a divinized son of God. Man's total entity, body, soul and spirit (the latter referring to God's Divine Life dwelling in man and man consciously corresponding by his "new life in Christ" to evolve this Life further) was to move in a continuous process of loving activities in the cosmos to a more conscious relationship to God. Man is called to enter into Divine Life and to become "partakers of the divine nature" (2 Pet. 1:4).

Vladimir Lossky gives the true mystical emphasis that is typical of Eastern Christian theology:

> Trinitarian theology is thus a theology of union, a mystical theology which appeals to experience, and which presupposes a continuous and progressive series of changes in created nature, a more and more intimate communion of the human person with the Holy Trinity.[2]

These Fathers saw God as constantly involved inside of the creative process through His "uncreated energies." Faced with the apparent paradox of God who is inaccessible and transcendent, yet God who loves His world and is continually communicating Himself to that world through man, made "according to the image and likeness of God," they taught that God relates to the outside world, above all, to us humans through His uncreated energies. These are not the essence of God that remains always inaccessible to the created world.

But God is present to man and creation in His energies. He is wholly unknowable in His essence, yet He is revealed to us in His energies. We can see therefore in this teaching that God never acts in us when we act "naturally" and then He begins to act in a different way, "supernaturally" when it is a question of grace. Grace in their views is primarily God in His energies touching man on all levels of his being out of His infinite, constant love in order to share Himself with mankind. The image that St. Gregory Palamas uses frequently to convey the distinction between God's essence and His energies is that of the sun and its rays. Given the sun, its rays are always going out to touch the outside world. The doctrine of the energies as distinct from the essence is the basis of all mystical experience.

The world therefore is constantly bathed in the grace of the divine energies. All is gift. All is grace. God does not simply create in a deistic fashion and let the world develop "naturally" by itself. Rather He continues to be involved, manifesting His love through his activating energies. Man can forget God. But God's energies are "uncreated." It is the total Trinity in dynamic, self-giving outwardly to man. There would never be a time when the world would be seen purely as "natural" without an ultimate finality that would be called "theosis," the divinization of man, and, through man's creative cooperation with God's energies, the spiritualization of the whole material world. Such Eastern Christian mystics by faith saw God continually acting in the whole world. A distinction that separated the sacred and the profane would be unthinkable for them.

In such a mystical vision the biblical accents on the transcendent and the immanent God are maintained in a workable antinomy. Through the doctrine of the uncreated energies God is seen as intimately related to his universe and still He is the God of Christian faith, the Trinity as perfect and complete in Itself.

THE VISION OF TEILHARD DE CHARDIN

A modern contemplative in action, the Jesuit scientist, Teilhard de Chardin, has captured well this dynamic presence of God inside His world and lovingly evolving it into greater consciousness with man's cooperation. Teilhard painstakingly in the *Phenomenon of Man* traces his vision of cosmogenesis from the first created proton to atoms, molecules, mineral, plant, animal and finally human life. Showing matter as moving always to higher forms of greater complexity in molecular structure, Teilhard shows that in man there is a proportionate development in consciousness. The law of complexity-consciousness leads Teilhard from out of the purely phenomenological level of scientific observation of nature in evolution to a hyperphysics that manifests itself in a planetary maturation which will finally climax at full, universal maturity, which point he calls Omega. On another level of speculation quite distinct from the above, Teilhard reflects through the psychology of the act of faith on the reasons that would make this ultimate point of ultra-humanity also a spiritual, autonomous, transcendent Person, Jesus Christ. On a third level, still quite distinct from the prior two reflections, Teilhard describes the Omega Point as the Prime Mover found in Holy Scripture, especially in the Gospel of St. John and the captivity letters of St. Paul.

In a stirring panoramic vision Teilhard joins the evolutionary process of nature with the Prime Mover fulfilling His salvific plan:

> The Parousia will undoubtedly take place when creation has reached the paroxysm of its capacity for union. The unique action of assimilation and synthesis which has been going on since the beginning of time will be revealed at last and the universal Christ will appear like a flash of lightning amid the clouds of a world which has gradually become sanctified ...The monads will rush to their irrevocable destiny...some, whose matter has been spiritualized, to the limitless fulfillment of eternal communion; others, whose spirit has become materialized, to the conscious agony of eternal decomposition.

> ...Like an immense wave, Being shall have dominated the agitation of beings. In the midst of a becalmed Ocean whose every drop of water shall be conscious of remaining itself, the extraordinary adventure of the world shall reach its term. The dream of every mystic shall have found its full and legitimate satisfaction. Erit in omnibus omnia Deus.[3]

WEAKNESSES OF TEILHARD'S VISION

In spite of the sweep and grandeur of Teilhard's vision that leaves us with a euphoric optimism knowing no bounds, we do sense some important questions left unanswered by Teilhard. Emile Rideau insists that Teilhard does not think out clearly the two moments of what belongs to history and what lies beyond history.[4]

At times Teilhard's optimism stresses the vision of St. Paul who unhesitatingly insists that, at the *Pleroma, en pasi panta Theos* ("That God may be all in all," 1 Cor. 15,28), Christ will draw all of humanity. "Some sort of unanimity will reign over the entire mass of the noosphere. The final convergence will take place in peace."[5]

Yet Teilhard, perhaps recalling Galileo's "e pur si muove," admits of another possibility. Although humanity would reach its fullness, individual human beings might not. He presents the "traditional, apocalyptic thinking" in his *Phenomenon of Man*:

> Refusal or acceptance of Omega? A conflict may supervene. In that case the noosphere, in the course of and by virtue of the processus which draws it together, will, when it has reached its point of unification, split into two zones, each attracted to an opposite pole of adoration. Thought has never completely united upon itself here below. Universal love would only vivify and detach finally a fraction of the noosphere so as to consummate it—the part which decided to 'cross the threshold,' to get outside itself into the other. . . .Not an indefinite progress, which is a hypothesis contradicted by the convergent nature of noogenesis, but an ecstasy transcending the dimensions and the framework of the visible universe. Ecstasy in concord; or discord; but in either case by excess of interior tension: the only biological outcome proper to or conceivable for the phenomenon of man.[6]

Teilhard, seemingly in his own thought, was caught in a quandary. On the one hand, he extrapolated the phenomenological, evolutionary process into the far future and saw that through the law of complexity-consciousness and ultra-humanity would converge through amorization as a cone to its point upon the Omega, Jesus Christ. Yet his traditional teaching Church insisted strongly that individuals would be free to abort the evolutionary process of noogenesis into Christogenesis. Thus two great weaknesses of Teilhard's system (he never comes to serious grips with the problems) are: 1) he fails to continue the evolutionary process beyond the Omega Point and 2) he does not answer how the majority of the human race, all those billions who have lived in the past, our present time and a good deal of the future to come, will reach the Omega Point?

Upon reaching the Omega Point, Teilhard's humanity bifurcates into two groups with rather unevolving, static conditions of eternal existence, Heaven or Hell. Love that was the cosmic force or energy propelling humanity to its Omega Point suddenly reaches a fixity that is of a totally unrecognizable quality from the personalizing love leading to the Omega Point.

In the light of these weaknesses, I would like to present some seminal ideas drawn from the Eastern Christian mystics. The life hereafter, based on knowledge and love of God or a lack of it, could be conceived in terms of a love of man for God and God for man, which would involve discovery in new knowledge, that would lead man to greater and greater love that would never reach full satiety.

In proposing some directional lines let us firstly keep in mind two points. The first stressed by C. S. Lewis in "The Great Divorce" reminds us of the mystery concerning the life hereafter:

All answers deceive. If you put the question (whether, as Paul seems to say that all men will be saved) from within time and are asking about possibility the answer is certain. The choice of ways is before you. Neither is closed. Any man may choose eternal death. But if you are trying to leap on into eternity, if you are trying to see the final state of all things as it will be when there are no more possibilities left, but only the Real, then you ask what cannot be answered to mortal ears. Time is the very lens through which you see—small and clear, as men see through the wrong end of a telescope, something that would otherwise be too big for you to see at all.[7]

The other point to be kept in mind is the basic conviction of us all, as Piet Schoonenberg points out in an essay entitled, "I believe in Eternal Life:"

A certain growth also remains possible in the final fulfillment. Otherwise we would perhaps cease to be human. Just as life constantly rediscovers itself from the past into the future, so we shall constantly rediscover our past and present in and from God in new and surprising ways.[8]

Before sketching some directional lines to the paradox of Omega Point and an evolving eschaton, permit me briefly to outline some provocative insights from two giants of the early Christian Church: Origen and Gregory of Nyssa, that might guide our thinking.

ORIGEN

I am not interested in developing all of his ideas on eschatology nor do I want to discuss the condemnation in the 2nd Council of Constantinople in 553 of his idea of *apokatastasis* or the final recapitulation wherein all human beings will reach salvation and Hell will go bankrupt. Convinced so absolutely of the perfection and constancy of God's love for all men, Origen, using highly mythical language (perhaps not in the least understood by his opponents), saw the redemptive action of Christ as a constant process in men through purification of their lower bodies (meaning entanglements with the corruptible and the temporal), until evil would be burned out of their hearts and then God would be all in all. Origen explains why he thinks that evil and matter, but not individuality, will be done away with eventually:

> Now I myself think that when it is said that God is 'all in all,' it means that he is also all things in each individual person. And he will be all things in each person in such a way that everything which the rational mind, when purified from all the dregs of its vices and utterly cleared from every cloud of wickedness, can feel or understand or think will be all God and that the mind will no longer be conscious of anything besides or other than God, but will think God and see God and hold God and God will be the mode and measure of its every movement; and in this way God will be all to it. For there will no longer be any contrast of good and evil, since evil nowhere exists; for God, whom evil never approaches, is then all things to it; nor will one who is always in the good and to whom God is all things desire any longer to eat of the tree of the knowledge of good and evil.[9]

Eventually, therefore, according to Origen all spirits, even the demons and Satan, will be saved and purified by the Logos. Origen knows of no eternal punishment. Since all beings came from God, His call will sound ever anew in their ears. Hans Lietzmann describes Origen's theology of the *eschaton* in these words:

They will trace his guidance in their lives, feel his parental hand in their suffering and need, a hand which will not abandon even the last creatures of all in the deepest regions of Hell. One after the other will be seized, accept conversion, mount slowly upwards joined by increasing numbers, and after inconceivable periods of time, the day will come when none will remain outside, and even when the prince of Hell will return to God. Then the 'return of the whole' will be completed, the purpose and meaning of the historical process fulfilled, death abolished, and Christ will place everything in himself and with himself at God's feet 'in order that God might be all in all.'[10]

GREGORY OF NYSSA

Gregory of Nyssa, who sought to purify the teachings of Origen on the pre-existence of souls, nevertheless seizes upon the truly positive insights of Origen and develops them further. A key insight taken from Origen is that the love of God in man is a force expanding his being and making him infinitely capable of possessing God in an unending process of greater growth.

True perfection Gregory describes as "never to stop growing towards what is better and never to place any limit on perfection."[11] Grace, or the life of God within man both in this life and the life to come, presupposes growth to accept a loving relationship with God. It is to accept the necessity of constantly moving toward God. He writes: "Seeing that it is of the nature of Goodness to attract those who raise their eyes towards it, the soul keeps rising ever higher and higher."[12]

Gregory gives us two reasons, still viable for us today, why man's progress toward God can never come to an end.

The first reason is that Beauty, God Himself, is infinite. The second is that the Beautiful is of such a nature that the desire for it can never be really satisfied.[13] Gregory writes: "The soul, that looks up towards God and conceives that good desire for His eternal beauty, constantly experiences an ever-new yearning for that which lies ahead and her desire is never given its full satisfaction."[14]

The soul ceases to mourn when she discovers "that the true satisfaction of her desire consists in constantly going on with her quest and never ceasing in her ascent, seeing that every fulfillment of her desire continually generates a further desire for the Transcendent."[15]

But if the good in man expands man's consciousness infinitely towards God, eventually that which is evil in man, his limited, distorted desires that man chooses in preference to God, will eventually be exhausted and man will turn towards God as the only source of perfection of man's true and ultimate good. For Gregory as for Origen evil was sin, a product of man's free choice and a loss of man's loving relationship with God. Evil was not a power conceived of as independently pitted against the good. Both affirmed that "the nonexistent could not exist forever."[16] In the process of *apokatastasis*, evil, which was not made by God and does not subsist in itself, must pass away, as man purified, comes to a greater knowledge and love of God. If evil were still to exist in being, then God could not be 'all in all.'

Finally, we might turn to Gregory for some insights on the problem of Hell. He describes Hell as a temporary process of purification:

. . .so also, when evil is being consumed by purifying fire, it is entirely necessary for the soul immersed in evil to be in the fire until the alien, earthly and counterfeit elements scattered through it are destroyed. . .The avenging flame will be more ardent the more it has to consume.[17]

Gregory gives no final opinion on the tragic problem of Hell. He saw the necessity from revelation that Hell as a condition of rebellion from God can exist and that it has eternal qualities (but measurement of eternity not to be imagined in terms of timelessness of our historical experience of time). He also saw as an absurdity the conceiving of anyone, made by God for God, who would reject indefinitely the goodness of God's love. The Church has constantly proclaimed that her saints have reached the state of Heaven; in her wisdom and humility she has never proclaimed anyone to be in Hell. Gregory realized that man reached full freedom only in choosing what conformed to his final destiny, i.e. God. Rejecting God, man chooses in a way that destroys or lessens his freedom. What this eternal fire of frustration meant for Gregory was limited by his insufficient notion of eternity. But Danielou suggests that it may also be from a certain awe, a tragic awe, before the mystery of human fulfillment in God's image through saying *yes* to God's love or the mystery of human frustration by saying *no*.

A MODERN ATTEMPT TO DESCRIBE
THE EVOLVING ESCHATON

What I offer for your consideration in this final section are some ideas that perhaps might serve both to break down our static theological constructs by a method of demythologizing as well as to replace them with more of a process-evolutionary approach. We have taken our human manner of conceiving body-soul, human freedom, death-judgment, heaven-hell as though these exist as objectivized, distinct creations existing in either a space-time continuum or in a life hereafter that is nothing more than a continuation of the same *chronos*, past, present, future time sequence that we know of in this life.

In our Western concept of man, the two constitutive parts of man are body and soul. Human freedom is conceived in terms of a choice between good and evil. Death is the violent separation of the soul from the body which latter goes into the coffin and is rejoined to the soul on a far distant day called the day of our resurrection. But immediately upon death, our soul stands before the all-knowing God who judges our life. We are given a reward of Heaven or an eternal punishment of Hell or assigned to an intermediate stage of Purgatory where we must satisfy the justice of God by expiation for sins not grave enough to sever our friendship with God. In Heaven or Hell, our state of bliss or punishment is fixed, this determined by the justice of God who, no matter how omnipotent He is and how infinite is His love for us, cannot, due to the demands of human freedom and His own justice, coerce our return of love. Justice demands no more mercy beyond the just conditions laid down by God at the beginning of the ball game.

Rather than expose the inadequacies of such out-moded conceptualization, may I be allowed to suggest some directional lines for future investigation? I would like to start with the biblical concept (hence Semitic, not Hellenistic) of man. St. Paul presents the biblical man as conceived by the Jewish people. He is composed of a body *soma* in Greek) that is for all purposes the whole man as a psycho-physical unity, a personality *ad extra*, in relation to the created, material world around him. Hence body-man is made up of the *soul* or *psyche* with all the emotions and passions that we call irascible and concupiscible as well as the *sarx* or the flesh.

The *pneuma* or spirit is the total man as viewed in his unique personality through a knowing relationship in love to God. Man is *this* individual person because God calls him by his personal name. Man becomes conscious of his own unique identity by relating in a love act to God as his ground of being. In the *soma* or body, man is in solidarity with the material world, with his environment. Man relates to the cosmic world through the body. Can we conceive of man as ever losing his body or his relation in solidarity to the material cosmos? The *pneuma* or spirit is a dynamic relation that, though also related to the changeable world of *chronos*, of time and space in matter, yet is more transcendent in its relationship to God in a conscious self-giving act of love towards God.

Death is a rather sudden disruption of man's relationship to the material world through the *sarx* or flesh. It is one of the most dramatic events in man's evolution, allowing man definitively to move into a greater consciousness through a dying to the vegetable and animal life in man.

Karl Rahner,[18] Paul Chauchard[19] and a host of other modern writers[20] wish to avoid separating the biblical *soma* or body from the soul. The whole person, the biblical *soma*, body-man, in his personality towards the world, now becomes more cosmically open to the whole universe. He becomes "all-cosmic" to use Rahner's expression. Death does not bring about a separation of the biblical body and soul, but it brings an end to our immersion in a lower stage of our evolutionary development, namely, the vegetable and animal level. Thus man in death moves higher to a greater complexity-in-consciousness where he now relates in greater intensity both *ad extra* to the cosmic world through an expanding awareness of his solidarity, both harmonious and disharmonious, with the material world and *ad intra* to a greater realization of his unique being in relationship to God.

THE RESURRECTION – A PROCESS

In the question of the resurrection of the body, could we not perhaps see it as a process, having already begun among those justified in Christ by a conscious Baptism, repeated in a commitment of growing intensity wherein man in his *pneuma* or spirit dies to an autonomy of self-love, rooted in the flesh and the passions, and yields to the everlasting *now* of the love of God towards him? The resurrection thus becomes an evolving event, not in the sequence of *chronos*, but in the spiritual determination of conscious love that Tillich and Cullmann call *kairos*, God's time, salvation-time, in which man opts to become truly human by answering to God's call within him. In this sense, the *soma*, with its body relations of man to the cosmos, rises into a higher participation of the life of the spirit. His *soma* becomes integrated with his *pneuma* so that as a total person he experiences the world in God and God in the world.

The Christian believes that Jesus Christ broke through the limitations of this human confinement to attain total enlightenment. He allowed His early followers a glimpse into His resurrectional presence. He came to them through closed doors, came upon some as they were walking. His body assumed different forms so they only gradually recognized Him in the breaking of the bread or through some other manifestation. As He could suddenly appear, so He could suddenly disappear.

St. Paul tells the Christians that this same Jesus will transfigure these poor bodies of ours into "copies of His glorious body" (Phil. 3,21). These bodies of ours sown now in corruptibility will pass into incorruptibility. Our glorified bodies will never more suffer or die. These bodies will enjoy a brilliance of body reflecting the spiritual wisdom then possessed. Jesus Christ had said, "The virtuous will shine like the sun in the Kingdom of their Father" (Matt. 13,43). The Book of Revelations describes it thus: "The Lord God will be shining on them. . .We shall be like Him because we shall see Him as He really is" (Rev. 22:5). Daniel earlier had said: "The learned will shine as brightly as the vault of heaven and those who have instructed many in virtue, as bright as stars for all eternity" (Dan. 12:2-3).

Our bodies will enjoy a subtlety that will continue to resist other material objects. They remain bodies but still are palpable and coexist with other bodies. They will enjoy an agility to move rapidly at the wish of the soul. And we will be present to as many persons as we have learned to love. St. Augustine has said: "We shall abide in such bodies that *wherever* we will to be and *whenever* we will to be, there we shall be."²¹ But St. John of the Cross highlights how love limits the body: "The soul lives where it loves rather than in the body which it animates, because it has not its life in the body, but rather gives it to the body and lives through love in that which it loves."[22] The moral perfection of love in this life will determine the degree of agility and presence to others in the life to come.

Once man has experienced an increase in conscious love of God for him and has returned that love in a true death-resurrection along the line of *kairos* or God's eternal *now* of self-sacrificing love, he enters into a new experience of freedom which may be difficult for us to understand. Freedom in loving God as the fullness of our being now consists in determining ourselves with the conscious totality of our being to choose Him rather than a self-centration. Could man say no to God? Yes, but this is not the same alternative as we faced on earth. Before the blazing truth that God infinitely loves us uniquely as individuals, we enter into our true freedom which now consists in determining ourselves to be the person we should be, a God-centered individual. We have no other criterion because we now clearly see our being tied completely to a loving relationship to God.

LIBERATING LOVE

The closest taste of this liberating freedom to *be* more uniquely ourselves by giving ourselves more totally and consciously to God is what we experience in true human love. It is neither degrading nor is it an imperfect freedom that allows us to choose not to love all others indiscriminately because we so completely want to love one worthy of our own self-giving. In this free determination we experience a true finding of ourselves, an expansion of our self-identity and a growth in complexity-consciousness. Not only do we feel our inward being has expanded, but we experience an openness to the outside world, a sense of greater solidarity that allows us to be of fulfilling service to others. In true unselfish human love, we approach closest to timelessness, to the eternal *now* of God's unselfish divine love. We are aware of a new level of existence, that, though still rooted in a material existence measurable in time and space, still transcends the perishable, the timely and moves into a consciousness that we feel could know no fatigue but also no end of further growth. True love, by its nature, is always creating within us a new capacity for greater love, which at the same time means a new capacity of *being* to give ourselves to another and a new capacity to receive *being* from the one loved.

Can we ever imagine therefore that our purified, unselfish love for God also would not enter into an ever increasing evolutionary process that would never know an end to knowledge of God or of loving surrender of self to God? Heaven is that condition wherein we exercise an ever increasing human freedom to determine to give ourselves to God and to God in His world. Redemption could perhaps better be conceived of as not a fixed state of beatific repose, but a growing process of discovering the love of God, both as manifested in His participated beauties in creation and as manifested by His direct revelation of Self to us.

THE PROBLEM OF HELL

But will all human beings eventually wake up in their roles as Prodigal Sons and return to the loving Father? Will the burning love of God cool the fires of frustration in the

hells created by individuals who have rejected God? We
have no human, objectivized answer to this mystery. The
New Testament presents us with a double picture that
seems contradictory. If we view each standpoint from the
same perspective: objectivized human time and human
values, we can only see a *cul de sac* with no resolution.

The first view from Holy Scripture asserts definitely
that there is a universal recapitulation process through
Christ in which all beings will be won to God.[23] St. Paul
especially insists on the resurrectional power of Christ to
recreate *all* men. "And when everything is subjected to
Him, then the Son Himself will be subject in His turn to
the One who subjected all things to Him so that God may
be all in all" (1 Cor. 15:28).

Again in his letter to Ephesians, Paul maintains that:
"He has put all things under His feet, and made Him, as
the ruler of everything, the head of the Church, which is
His body, the fullness of Him who fills the whole creation"
(Ephes. 1:22-23). And in Romans 5:18, he claims: "Again,
as one man's fall brought condemnation on everyone, so
the good act of one man brings everyone life and makes
them justified."

In contrast we find the other view of a world divided
into sheep and goats, the saved and the damned, Heaven
and Hell. This Hell is of everlasting fire as the text of Matt.
25 pictures it.

Can these two views be reconciled? As long as we
project our vision of *chronos*, our human objectivization,
upon this picture, the choice before man is either/or. For
man choosing, salvation is truly either God or no God.
Either a choice of love and happiness with God and in God
or an infinitely, everlasting fire of human frustration. But
as Emil Brunner points out in his short work, *The*

Divine-Human Encounter,[24] we create a theological ship-wreck by reducing to objective concepts that which is so personal and unique that it can be discovered only in the intimacy of a love experience with a *Thou*. Why must human freedom be objectivized so that it becomes opposed to the omnipotence of God? We should, however, learn to see freedom, as was hinted at earlier, as a privilege, an opening to new complexity, greater richness in being, a movement towards realizing by inter-subjective possession that which our whole being yearns for.

We might be able to see this as applied to those beings who have "tasted and seen how sweet the Lord is." A trained pianist enjoys his work and his skill increases as well as his enjoyment as he wants more and more to play. He is now not forced; he wants to play because he has experienced an enrichment. The person loving God wants to do so more and more.

But what about the person in Hell? Can he be free and God be omnipotent and still both be reconciled? It is here that we must refuse with Christ to answer this question posed in Luke 13,23: "Master, will the elect be few in number? Christ replied only: "Strain every nerve to enter by the narrow door." For man making the great decision and for Christ and every preacher concerned with exhorting man in this life to choose rightly, Hell is possible. It is eternal. It is everlasting fire. It is irreversible. It is beyond man's freedom to change his decision. He can choose in this earthly life; his choice, as far as his human powers go to change it, is irrevocable. Hell is a most real possibility as man makes his choice in this life and it is everlasting frustration.

GOD WILLS THE SALVATION OF ALL

But from Christ's side, in the realm, not of objectivization that might induce man, making his earthly choices, to rely with foolhardy presumption upon an unlimited mercy of God, but in the realm of the human-divine encounter between God and man, the *I* and *Thou*, there is another perspective that is of a totally different nature. Man cannot alter his eternal loss; he can only exist in an everlasting pain of being deprived of God. But from God's viewpoint, the Gospel message tells us that God wants and wills that all men be saved. For God to will the salvation of all men is for God continuously to love each man in a unique, personal encounter. What is humanly unbelievable that God is love for us has happened in Jesus Christ. In the words of St. Paul to the Philippians: "His state was divine, yet He did not cling to His equality with God but emptied Himself to assume the condition of a slave" (Phil. 2:6-7). "Yes, but He was crucified through weakness, and still He lives now through the power of God" (2 Cor. 13:4). Understanding and succumbing to God's incarnated love for man in Jesus Christ to the kenotic point of giving Himself totally, even to the death of the Cross, Paul considers the greatest and only ultimate knowledge that contains all other knowledge is to "know nothing except Jesus Christ and Him crucified" (1 Cor. 2,2).

Origen beautifully describes the filling up of the sufferings of Christ as Christ remaining on the Cross as long as one sinner remains in Hell.[25] Christ's love act on the Cross is an everlasting act in *kairos*, timelessness, in the eternal now, that knows no end until man answers with a return of love. "I, if I be lifted up from the earth, will

draw all men unto Myself" (Jn. 12,32). God makes known
to individual humans His infinite, personal love for us
through the humanized love of Christ on the Cross. A
parable suggested by John A. T. Robinson might be
helpful. He describes in the following way God's wearing
down of man's resistance or, better, of man entering into
true freedom of self-determination to love God in a total
commitment of self.[26]

To everyman eternally there are opened two ways.
One road, crowded, full of people, leads to destruction.
The other leads to true freedom in a conscious surrender
of self to God. Somewhere along the first road, far or near
from its beginning, man meets Someone, a figure, stooping
beneath the weight of the Cross. "Lord, why are You
doing this?" each of us sometime or other asks. "For you,
to prove that you are greatly loved by God." No man can
indefinitely meet such great love, especially in his bitter
emptiness and loneliness of self-love and continue to resist.
Man will not lose his choice to resist. He will want, like a
feverish thirsting man on a desert, to stretch out to drink
of this life-giving water. Paul says: "For God's foolishness
is wiser than human wisdom, and God's weakness is
stronger than human strength" (Cor. 1:25). It is a
fundamental paradox that only omnipotence can afford to
become so weak, so humiliated in pursuing man so
relentlessly like the Hound of Heaven.

God is God precisely because He is the perfection of
all that we are in our limited possibilities. And man's
greatest, most free, most human act is to love another
unselfishly. If we return love for love in this life or in the
continued evolving life to come, it is not because we have
first loved God, but because, first and last, in the alpha or
the omega of our true, human conscious, adult life, He,

God, omnipotent in His humility, has, or better, He *is* ever loving us.

THE THERAPY OF PURGATORY

The doctrine of Purgatory, that there is a period of purification for those who have died in the Lord, is in great need of further doctrinal development. The early Church Fathers, both Greek and Latin, held that there was a period of purification of the "relics" of sinfulness in some Christians who could be helped by the prayers of the faithful. St. Augustine especially, using the texts from 1 Cor. 3:13-15 and Matt. 12:32, allowed that certain sinners may attain pardon in the world to come by undergoing purification through purgatorial fire.[27]

The Eastern Fathers avoided the thorny problem of merit and expiation through temporal punishment of fire and held, without much precision, that there was an intermediate stage before the final judgment. In this intermediate stage the departed would come to know their partial ignorance. They would feel their attachment to themselves over an absolute submission in all things to God. If in this life in moments of conversion we can shed tears and be filled with remorse for having lived so many years of our lives without a deep, pure love for God, how much more in the after-life when we will no longer be tied to the binding dispersion of matter and localized in space. Our spiritual powers will give us a new consciousness of who we are and who God is. The past will be present just as though it were happening. Above all, God will be shown to us in His beauty through communion with other human beings, both in Heaven and those still living on earth.

THE COMMUNION OF THE SAINTS

When the Church is vibrant with deeply contemplative Christians, the understanding of the communion
between the living and the dead is a great reality. The
mystic lives on a deeper plane of reality so he sees no great
chasm separating himself both in this life from his living
neighbors for whom day and night he stands before the
throne of God interceding. He feels united also in prayer
with all the saints, angels and those not quite brought into
the fullness of God's glory, even those in the state of
complete alienation from God, in the state of Hell.

The love of Christ in the contemplative burns to win
all to Christ. One wants to share the riches of Christ with
all. If St. Paul, while on earth burned with a desire to
become all things to all men to win them for Christ, how
much more does St. Paul in Heaven burn with the love of
Christ in him to intercede for all of us? The Church has
always taught doctrinally and devotionally in the cult to
the saints and through the liturgical prayers on behalf of
the saints that there is communication between the living
in this life and those living in Christ in the life after death.

From the very beginning the Church honored the
memory of those who died in Christ. The faithful were
sure that the mutual contact they enjoyed by praying for
each other when alive could not be broken even by death.
Origen speaks often of martyrs who stand before the altar
of God like angels to support our prayers. P. Styger in his
excavations of the catacombs of San Sebastiano in Rome
has brought to light graffiti of the 3rd century scratched
on stone by pilgrims to the graves of Sts. Peter and Paul to
obtain their intercession.

It is interesting to note that in the Byzantine Liturgy

of St. John Chrysostom the priest prays: "Moreover we offer You this spiritual and bloodless sacrifice for our forefathers in the faith who have gone to their rest, for the fathers, patriarchs, prophets, apostles, preachers, evangelists, martyrs, confessors, ascetics and for every just soul that has died in the faith. . . .And especially for our most holy, most pure, most blessed and glorious Lady, the Mother of God and ever-virgin Mary." This prayer has meaning in the light of the Christian faith-vision that the faithful gather to celebrate the Liturgy in union with the Heavenly courts of angels and saints and all those who have died in the faith of Christ. The many icons throughout a Byzantine church, on the iconostasis or screen that separates the people from the Holy of Holies, on stands, on the walls, up above in the cupolas, call the faithful vividly to this realization of the Church Militant uniting with the Church Triumphant and the Church Suffering (in the after-life). All are members of the Body of Christ, but each group manifests a different level of "life in Christ." Such prayers for Mary the Mother of God and the saints of old could mean that the faithful implore God that the blessed may join with the living faithful in this liturgical sacrifice. It is also a prayer of thanksgiving to God for their glory and victory. It is also a plea that the Lord have mercy on the praying community that asks this through the saints' intercession.

If the saints therefore continue to be active, with full consciousness, memory and understanding of our needs and can exercise acts of love and compassion towards us still in this exile, what does this important teaching of the communion of the saints have still to tell us? Would it be beyond our Christian faith to believe that the saints therefore through their loving concern for us in our many needs can actually grow in greater love? Can one who loves God in the life to come not want to share that love, even to want to become involved with those in greatest need? Each act of love, each concerned thought for one of us on this earth by one who knows the Lord "face to face" should push that person to a new level of human growth, of human consciousness of God's beauty both in himself and in the life of the one for whom the saint interceded.

Man would cease being human, made "according to the image and likeness of God," if he could not grow continuously towards infinity in ever-increasing love. If he finally met the Omega in a completed state of fixity, what would love of God and neighbor mean in such a vacuum? Yet what an injustice that the habitual image used of eternal happiness is that of a long, eternal sleep! "Eternal rest grant unto them, O Lord," the Requiem Mass for centuries resounded. But the reality should show man both in this life and the next progressing continually through the love of the Holy Spirit indwelling to become more and more transformed through the knowledge and contemplative experience of knowing God in Himself and in all of His works, especially other human beings and of being personally known and loved by Him both directly and by His loveableness in all of His saints.

HEAVEN IS TO GROW IN LOVE

One of the incisive insights that many of the Eastern Christian mystics such as Origen, St. Gregory of Nyssa and St. Gregory of Nazianzus, St. Maximus the Confessor and St. Symeon the New Theologian, to name only a few, give us is the idea of continued progress for humans in the life to come. For those in Heaven perfection does not consist in possession, in rest, because they have already participated in God's love that is illimitable. Since God's beauty that beckons man on is limitless, the desire in man must be also limitless. Would this not introduce frustration into Heaven? St. Gregory of Nyssa seeks to explain the tension between motion and stability:

> ...if nothing comes from above to intercept its flight, seeing that it is of the nature of Goodness to attract those who raise their eyes towards it, the soul keeps rising ever higher and higher, stretching with its desire for heavenly things to those that are before (Phil. 3:13), as the Apostle tells us, and thus it will always continue to soar ever higher. For because of what it has already attained, the soul does not wish to abandon the heights that lie beyond it. And thus the soul moves ceaselessly upwards, always reviving its tension for its onward flight by means of the progress it has already realized. Indeed, it is only spiritual activity that nourishes its force by exercise; it does not slacken its tension by action but rather increases it.[28]

True vision of God for St. Gregory is that the soul that looks upon God never ceases to desire Him. At the heart of man's love for God is always service. We see Mary, the Mother of God, declared full of grace by the Angel Gabriel when she consented and gave her *fiat* to serve the Lord (Lk. 1:38) as His handmaid. How she must have grown in that love as she served the Word made flesh in the 30 years at Nazareth! At the foot of the cross, how that grace, that surrendering love reached its fullest desire to possess and be possessed by that Word! And after 2,000 human years, according to the reckoning of earth-men, what must *now*, in her presence to Jesus Christ and her desire to serve Him in all the children of God, be her fullness of grace!

I often think of the parallel of a mother with a retarded child. How the retarded child calls out more love from the mother than the mother is challenged to give to her other "normal" children! Her love is so unselfish and yet any such mother will tell the world how much she has received in real growth in love and human self-realization.

I hardly would like to argue from such an example to an objective reality about which we can know very little until we too enter into the life to come. But it seems that it would not be a heretical position in the light of the constant tradition of the Church that has believed from earliest times that Mary, Mother of God, has been assumed bodily into Heaven and that she is constantly interceding for God's children, especially, is she concerned with those in greatest need. The most retarded children of God are those who objectively have never known the beauties of Jesus Christ or have never grasped "the breadth and the length, the height and the depth" of the love of Christ.

HEAVEN—A COMMUNITY OF LOVE

As I grow older in my priestly ministry, the more I become compassionate towards sinners who come to be healed in the sacrament of reconciliation. I begin to see the awfulness of sin as a darkening of man's ability to see God because one individual was forced to grow up in a broken family and at an early age was on the streets in gangs who knew only violence and hatred for the moneyed-class; another was spoiled by wealthy parents and never knew self-discipline, only self-indulgence. One other was brought up on an Irish Jansenism that feared sex. I ask how much their sins are deliberate acts of turning away from God and how much was their society responsible. The evident truth is that here are broken people who want the healing love of Jesus Christ.

When I ponder the power of culture to keep a whole nation tied to a religion that militates against Christianity or that has experienced, as a colony of so-called Christian colonial nations, Christianity as a religion of the "ruling" and exploiting class, then I ask: "Lord, what about the billions in history who through society's limitations never had a chance to know you?"

If society and groups of individuals are so powerful in shaping the acts and values of individual human beings, would not God in His mercy allow a new society, His Church Triumphant, be the means to reveal His compassion for them and lead them from the level of love that they attained during their lives through free, grace-ladened acts of self-giving to others? Man dies and brings into eternity that level of consciousness as a human being that he has reached throughout his human existence by making choices in accord with his conscience. If the Church's doctrine about Purgatory has any truth to it, it would mean that a therapy is at work in the life to come for those who have not totally separated themselves from God.

St. Augustine used the following text to show that some sins are expiated in the life to come. "Every one of men's sins and blasphemies will be forgiven, but blasphemy against the Spirit will not be forgiven. And anyone who says a word against the Son of Man will be forgiven; but let anyone speak against the Holy Spirit and he will not be forgiven either in this world or in the next" (Matt. 12:31).

Can we not believe that the saints and even our loved

ones who are still attached to us, even though they have entered into their purification process before us, not only will help us, but in a real way they need us in order to allow their great love for God to unfold and be actualized in a new, expanded consciousness. They are like those who have graduated with their Ph.D. degrees and are teaching us on this earth how to read, write and do simple problems. All who believe in Jesus Christ are living members of His Body and this presence to each member transcends the temporal and spatial limitations of our imperfect existence on this earth. Milton professes this belief in his verse:

> Millions of spiritual creatures walk the Earth unseen, both when we wake and when we sleep.

Some day we will understand how our loved ones, also the angels and saints, were most influential in helping us to love God while we were on this earth. My earthly father passed away a year ago. But God has gifted me with such a vivid realization of his living presence with me throughout the whole day, especially when I celebrate the Liturgy daily, that I can hardly lament the fact of his departure from this life but praise God that he has died in the Lord and he has now become the contemplative that God calls all of us to be.

CONTEMPLATION IS LOVE

True contemplation and sanctity both in this life and in the life to come must be measured exclusively by the degree of charity and humility possessed by the individual.

The love of God within us, experienced in deep contemplation, "urges" us, to use St. Paul's strong term, to go out from ourselves in humble service to all who need God's healing love, especially to our closest loved ones and to those who are in most desperate need. This, it seems to me, is of the essence of our Christian vocation. And Heaven should be no exception to this standard of Christian excellence. We know whether God is in us by the love that we have for one another. True contemplation is always begetting, becoming the other in greater unity of love that alone can be realized by humble service, inter-relational involvement of self-giving toward the other.

This is shown in the belief of many holy persons while still in this life. St. Dominic promised his confreres that he would be more useful to them after his death than while he was still living. St. Therese of Lisieux wanted to remain seated at the table of sinners in her solidarity with them. She promised to help her missionary friends more in Heaven than she did through her prayers and sacrifices while on earth. The sacrifice of oneself in place of others is at the heart of Christianity. "A man can have no greater love than to lay down his life for his friends," said the Master Himself (Jn. 15:13). As He did on the Cross in imitation of the kenotic love of His Heavenly Father towards each of His children, so His Holy Spirit inspires His disciples that the only sign whereby people will recognize them as His followers is by the love they have for one another, for all men.

LOVE ALONE REMAINS AND GROWS

St. Paul assures us that in the life to come all other things will pass away except love. "Love does not come to

an end" (1 Cor. 13:8). For those who have already entered
into eternity, the earth is where God is present and His
presence is growing. The Body of Christ is being formed
here on earth. But again St. Paul assures us that the
healthy members of the body come to the aid of any
injured or needy members. "If one part is hurt, all parts
are hurt with it. If one part is given special honor, all parts
enjoy it" (1 Cor. 12:26). Does this not imply a loving
involvement of all healthy members? Without exaggeration
can we not believe that our beloved relatives and friends in
Heaven seek to help us grow in greater happiness in Christ?
Not only do they help us, then, but we must help them by
bringing them joy through our successes. We too as healthy,
praying members can help them grow stronger in Christ if
they are in need of greater charity. Now they are in a
position to know the true love that we had for them in the
past and now in the present and our love for them makes
them stretch out with greater love for God in us and in
them.

And it boggles the mind of the contemplative to
think not only of how we shall grow in loving our relatives
and friends in greater depth than the superficial beginnings
started in this life but also how we shall come to know in
an eternity awaiting us all the billions of humans and
angels created by God and in whose lives God has been so
active in loving them through the billions and billions of
creatures that He has given them in His personalized,
loving activities throughout all of their existence!

Heaven will hardly be an old folks' home! But it will
be a dynamic interaction of love as we discover God in His
unique love for each person that we encounter, both in
Heaven and on earth and even in Purgatory and in Hell, all
conceived no longer as places caught in a time-space

continuum. We will positively allow the power of God in Christ Jesus through His ever-present Gift of His Holy Spirit to interact in all of us so that our power to love increases. We grow as the love of God in us grows. The Body of Christ grows more full of grace. It stretches forth to actualize under God's uncreated energies of love not only the potential in each human being, but through our loving interaction to touch also the whole material universe and bring it also into the Body of Christ.

Thus the healthy members of the Body of Christ in Heaven remain concerned with this earth. "For He must be King until He has put all His enemies under His feet and the last of the enemies to be destroyed is death, for everything is to be put under His feet" (1 Cor. 15:26). This is an active love on the part of the saints seeking to wipe out any misery. How God revealed this mystery to such a little one as St. Therese of Lisieux who wrote: "What draws me towards the Heavenly Fatherland is the call of the Lord, the hope of finally being able to love Him as I have so much desired to love Him and the thought that I will be able to make a multitude of souls love Him and bless Him for all eternity. . .I wish to spend my Heaven doing good on earth."

A favorite author of mine, Georges Bernanos, has made this sense of solidarity with sinners, to the point of voluntary substitution, the basis of true Christian holiness. He rather dramatically and even romantically pushes this kind of substitution in the experience of damnation in imitation of Christ on the Cross. But H. Urs von Balthasar has interpreted the theology of Bernanos in terms of ultimate love of Christ in the mystic conquering him to the point of "folly" in order to lead others to Christ. He writes:

We have reached here the antipodes of that ascending
contemplation, of the individualistic type, which has been
more markedly impressed by the Neo-Platonist stamp than by
the spirit of the Gospel, which has wormed its way through
the patristic and scholastic tradition, and which, even today,
still constitutes the mystical schema highly favored in certain
famous schools of theology. As far as Bernanos is concerned,
true mysticism "does not resemble that which we read in
books" (*La Joie*, pg. 230). It consists simply in this: that one
allows himself to be thrown out of all shelter, not only out of
worldly shelters, but even far away out of that supernatural
security of the life of faith as guaranteed by the Church
herself. The true mystic is a man who lets himself be cast
down into the abyss, where he is tossed about in all directions,
in a kind of darkness where there is no distinction between up
and down, for to be forsaken by the Father is to be delivered
into the hands of Satan.[29]

In Heaven the saints no longer see Jesus Christ by
faith but face-to-face. Still, although they know they could
never be damned out of love for Christ, their love must
stretch itself to such heights of "folly"because of the great
love unto folly that they have experienced coming from
Jesus Christ. The more one is raised to this life in Christ,
the more he enters into communion with all other human
beings. There develops within him a genuine sense of being
one with the whole world, created by God and loved by
God as good. He is open and ready to give himself to this
world and more specifically to the needy in that world.
True love of God must make all of us into active lovers of
all other human beings. "As long as we love one another,
God will live in us and His love will be complete in us. . ."
(1 Jn. 4:8).

We believe that Christ will come at the end of time

(in the *Parousia*) to transform this universe by bringing it to its completion in and through Himself. But in a real sense, the *Parousia*, the appearance of Christ in glory, is already present in our universe for persons of deep prayer. Their faith and hope and love in Jesus Christ allows them in this life on earth to pull aside the veil in order to see, in the beautiful words of Teilhard de Chardin, "Jesus Christ, shining diaphanously through the whole world." He is now achieving the victory over cosmic evil through all of his members on earth and those living in Him in eternal life. He is precisely overcoming the forces of death, sin and chaos and is bringing about a gradual transfiguration of the entire creation of God. But this transfiguration process, since it is energized by God's very own uncreated energies of love living inside His alive members, will stretch forth, always resting in the freshness of the love acquired and enjoyed in contemplation; yet always restless to love more by serving those who are in great need of His love.

How beautifully St. Paul captures the freshness of this new creation in Christ Jesus and yet the need for continued reconciliation unto Him:

> And for anyone who is in Christ, there is a new creation; the old creation has gone, and now the new one is here. It is all God's work. It was God who reconciled us to Himself through Christ and gave us the work of handing on this reconciliation. In other words, God in Christ was reconciling the world to Himself, not holding men's faults against them, and He has entrusted to us the news that they are reconciled. So we are ambassadors for Christ; it is as though God were appealing through us, and the appeal that we make in Christ's name is: be reconciled to God. For our sake God made the Sinless One into sin, so that in Him we might become the goodness of God (2 Cor. 5:17-21).

God is becoming God as we become signs of the new creation by the love we allow to shine forth from our lives into the lives of others. God will always be evolving more and more into Love made manifest in Christ Jesus by the love of God in us allowing us with God's energy to love others. The contemplative who has learned even in this life to enter deeply into his heart and there surrender completely in humble, loving service to God's Word experiences that he has entered into this growing, dynamic process and that nothing of death or sin can have a part in his life once he has begun to experience the energizing power of God's love within his life. He is oriented outward, towards others, to give this love of God to all whom he meets. Heaven is truly within him and he thirsts for more of this life-giving water that is God's personalized Love, the Holy Spirit, brooding over the earth and the heavens, impatient to bring forth the life of Christ in all things.

Such a contemplative sees himself and the whole material world as a unity, "as beautiful as a bride all dressed for her husband" (Rev. 21:2). He has his feet planted on this earth and yet he stands before the throne of God. He receives daily the Word of God calling out from the throne:

> You see this city? Here God lives among men.
> He will make His home among them; they shall be
> His people, and He will be their God; His name
> is God-with-them. He will wipe away all tears
> from their eyes; there will be no more death and
> no more mourning or sadness. The world of the
> past has gone.
> Then the One sitting on the throne spoke:
> 'Now I am making the whole of creation new,'

He said, 'Write this: that what I am saying
is sure and will come true.' And then He said,
'It is already done. I am the Alpha and the
Omega, the Beginning and the End. I will give
water from the well of life free to anybody who
is thirsty; it is the rightful inheritance of
the one who proves victorious; and I will be his
God and he a son to Me (Rev. 21:3-7).

APPENDIX

Mysticism and Occultism

Five years ago a group of Protestant charismatic men, members of one of the chapters of the Full Gospel Businessmen's Fellowship on the East Coast, approached me with an admonition. I had a few weeks before been the guest speaker at the monthly prayer supper, but two weeks later some of the members came upon a brochure advertising an ecumenical yoga retreat that I was giving with an Indian swami and a Jewish rabbi. "How could you do such a thing?" they asked me. "After such a beautiful witness to Jesus Christ that you gave us, then you turn around and publicly admit to practising yoga."

I asked them whether they knew what yoga was and they confessed that they really didn't know but they were sure it was diabolical. "Our people believe this yoga along with practising those Far Eastern religions is a part of occultism." I tried to explain how I have been using the hatha yoga postures for years precisely as a means, a help to deeper prayer and greater union with Jesus Christ. I could see that I was confronting a prejudice of long standing which I have since encountered in direct confrontation with "charismatic" leaders, both among Protestant and Catholic charismatic groups. Occasionally I have found written tracts issuing general fulminations against such things as occultism, magic, necromancy, ESP, drugs, yoga and transcendental meditation, all put into the same category and summarily dismissed by a few texts from Scripture.

The Book of Deuteronomy clearly taught them: "There must never be anyone among you who makes his son or daughter pass through fire, who practises divination, who is soothsayer, augur or sorcerer, who uses charms, consults ghosts or spirits, or calls up the dead. For the man who does these things is detestable to Yahweh your God" (Deut. 18:10-12). Saul and the witch of Endor are quoted (1 Sam. 28:7-25) along with (Lev. 19:31;21:6,27).

A built-in fundamentalism, fear of mysticism and a spirit of anti-scientism can account largely for this stance among conservative Protestants and Catholics.

Representative of the literature that circulates among such groups is the following from the well-known Chinese Pentecostal author, Watchman Nee:

> Today's so-called scientific hypnotism and religious yogi, which enable people to possess the powers of telepathy, healing, and transforming, are in reality founded upon two principles. Using the argument that certain methods can be beneficial to mankind, those of this class who perform such techniques as focusing one's attention, sitting silently, contemplating and meditating are actually employing these devices to reduce their mind to a blank condition and their will to passivity so as to invite supernatural spirits or demons to supply them with many wonderful experiences. . . .We simply wish to acquaint the Lord's children with the principles behind practice of black arts; which are a blank and passive mind and will. Evil spirits are overjoyed should these conditions be

present, as they can immediately commence to do their dark work.

The basic distinction between the operating requirements of the Holy Spirit and the wicked spirits can be summarized as follows:

1. All supernatural revelations, visions or other strange occurrences which require total cessation of the function of the mind, or are obtained only after it has ceased working, are not of God.
2. All visions which arise from the Holy Spirit are conferred when the believer's mind is fully active. It necessitates the active engagement of the various functions of the mind to apprehend these visions. The endeavor of evil spirits follow exactly the opposite course.
3. All which flows from God agrees with God's nature and the bible.[1]

I have given this extensive quotation both because it summarizes the standard teaching in such Pentecostal circles and also because Watchman Nee is so widely read. What is at stake here is more than whether Christians can play with ouija boards and commune with the dead. The defense of a legitimate Christian mysticism is here at stake. I would be so bold as to say this issue is striking at the fundamental differences between a true biblical anthropology of man's nature as interpreted correctly by the whole tradition of the Eastern Fathers and that interpreted by the Augustinianism of Martin Luther and John Calvin.

In the latter view, in fighting a Pelagian position that man could gain Heaven by his own efforts, man's nature, stripped of God's grace by sin, is seen as a *massa damnata.* Nature and all of mankind are corrupt and there is nothing good to be found there. In comparison, the vision from Holy Scripture of the Greek Fathers that man has been created by God "according to God's image and likeness" is optimistic. Each man, in spite of sin, possesses deep down within his spiritual powers a basic goodness that allows man always the possibility of answering the call of God uttered within the depths of man's being to become consciously a son of God by the grace of Jesus Christ given man through His Holy Spirit. Man is not totally corrupt! And for the Christian he firmly believes that by Baptism and a constant, daily correspondence with the grace of that Baptism, received through Jesus Christ and His Holy Spirit, his "inner man" is to grow into the utter fullness of God. The Holy Trinity truly dwells within the Christian. Man's body is a temple of God. Man needs only to turn within his inner self and by faith he finds His adorable God.

MYSTICISM IS NOT OCCULTISM

Mysticism is not the same as occultism. The Christian's end of his life is to contemplate God in all things. Man is made not only to adore the transcendent God outside of himself by keeping His commandments. He is made also to turn within himself and find the uncreated energies of the loving Trinity divinizing man into a greater and greater conscious relationship of likeness to Jesus Christ in whom every man has his *raison d'être*, his ultimate reason for being.

If Christianity limits itself only to an awesome, terrifying God, outside man and approached only by fear, then the Incarnation never has taken place. But Jesus Christ, risen, dwells within our hearts. He is constantly releasing the Holy Spirit who divinizes us, making us true participators of God's very own nature by grace (2 Pet. 1:4). Man must hear God also saying from the depths of his being: "Be still and know that I am God" (Ps. 46:10, KJV). We must not fear silence. It is not the same as utter passivity, quietism or vacuity.

Watchman Nee's injunction that a Christian must never be still and meditate because one opens himself up to the demonic who will then take over and possess our consciousness militates against any higher degree of contemplation beyond a busy absorption in Holy Scripture. Holy Scripture is a living word and, rather than turn away from it in an empty quietism, the Christian, by entering into his "heart," allows the Holy Spirit to reveal the inner riches of Scripture in ways beyond man's reasoning.

A REAL DANGER

There is another important caution about deeper contemplation that is more existential than the reason given by fundamentalists. When a person does move into deeper prayer through years of accompanying asceticism through which he strives to bring his heart into a purity and docility to the inner presence of God indwelling, the contemplative more and more yields his own activity, especially on a discursive level, to that of the immanent presence of God. This is not to say he is completely passive and surrendering his will. The Christian in any stage of prayer, even ecstasy of the highest order, is self-directing. He wills to surrender himself to God's activity. He actively becomes receptive, the highest form of immanent action and human freedom. Faith is always operating. This is the loving receptivity of Jesus Christ in His earthly prayer on the mountain top at night to His Heavenly Father. It is the prayer-form we shall enjoy in Heaven where knowledge will be intuitional and not discursive.

POSSIBLE DANGERS

True contemplation cannot be attained unless there be a deep, inner silence and stillness. Part of that stillness comes from stilling our own mental activity and waiting humbly and in deep faith that the immanently dwelling God will speak. To pass beyond the superficial levels of our own controlled consciousness in order to pass into the innermost core of our being, great discipline is required. But as one does pass through layers of psychic experiences, danger zones rear up. The "voyager" into the interior passes into waters filled with hidden rocks ready to capsize the small sailing vessel. Repressed material that has been drowned in the unconscious can rise threateningly to disturb the one in prayer. Sexual feelings can arise, even influencing our whole body and bringing us close to move over to see the strange faces of the demonic that flash now brilliantly, now darkly from within.

Flashes and lights, psychic powers of telepathy, communing with the dead can come forth. What is reality, what is hallucination before the beckoning visions of enticing forms that whirl over the screen of our consciousness? Voices that we recognize and strange voices give their messages with impelling realism. Again, what is real, what is false? The rocks of Scylla and Charybdis come close and I could capsize. Do I withdraw or push deeper?

I have known Christians who have given up Christ and spent several years in India meditating daily for hours under the guidance of a Hindu guru who felt they had unleashed powers within themselves that they could hardly control. This summer a veteran yoga meditator in Ohio went into a trance over a weekend and never returned to this life. He wanted to project himself as far as he could, "astrally." The demonic is within all of us. We carry within our minds psychic power undreamed of. Only in Heaven will we understand what potential is really locked within our minds and that both for good and evil. But because such powers can be dangerous and the evil spirits can enter and manipulate us if we passively yield to their presence is no reason why we should avoid deeper prayer.

NEED TO OPEN THE UNCONSCIOUS TO BE HEALED

We are more than our habitual consciousness reveals us to be. Deep within the various levels of our consciousness and unconscious lie parts of us that we perhaps would never recognize. But because we refuse to open these areas up to our conscious gaze and seek healing from the Lord, we repress these areas. The many fears, anxieties, moods of anger, depression and hatred that come upon us from no apparent outside cause are indications of a smoldering volcano lying deep beneath the surface of our habitual knowledge of self.

Today God has revealed much about the workings of the human psyche through the discoveries made in depth-psychology and psycho-therapy. One of Carl Jung's commentators, Dr. Ira Progoff,[2] compares the psyche to a cross-sectional drawing of geologic rock formation. At the top is a thin layer of surface rock that we call consciousness. Below this is a thicker layer of rock that we can call the personal unconscious. Underlying both of these layers there is a dark, volcanic base extending back to the very core of the earth itself, bringing the individual into primordial contact with all of creation as a part to a whole. This Jung calls the collective unconscious or conscience of the Universal Man. Occasionally out of this volcano there erupt materials that rise to the surface, passing through the other layers.

If man is to enter into an integrated personality, to harmonize all the various levels of psychic life within man's mind, (Jung calls this process: *individuation*), the upper layers of the psyche must be harmonized with the lower layers. This means that the lower layers must be opened up to the scrutiny of the consciousness. Man will always remain crippled and a victim of primordial factors in his life unless he opens up these lower layers.

In the charismatic renewal much stress is placed on the healing of memories. This is a powerful way of relaxing within the context of a communal prayer service so that an individual can bring to his consciousness the hidden material lying in his unconscious layers and through his enlivened faith he can see his fragmentation and alienation from his true self in Christ and cry out for healing. He asks that each person he has injured in the past may be healed. That he himself may be healed in the areas of injury received from a lack of love from others. He prays that any hidden resentment or unforgiveness in him towards others may be dissolved by the love of the Holy Spirit pouring over these hidden areas of repressed bitterness.

Among Catholics the sacrament of Penance is a powerful healing of the inner recesses of one's consciousness and unconscious. What needs to be emphasized in the reception of this sacrament is the necessity of the penitent to enter deeply into his being and expose his wounds in their root sources. How few of us have sufficient self-knowledge of the movements of our hearts to confess our need of healing in specific areas! Erich Fromm, one of the leading contemporary psychoanalysts, boldly makes the statement that "most of what people have in their conscious minds is fiction and delusion. . .therefore consciousness as such has no particular value."[3]

It is only when we are at peace and tranquil, when we pass from an *alpha* level of brain activity, as biofeedback terms the switch from our busy mental activity (*beta* level), to enter into a more creative level when our consciousness is led down into other layers of our true self that new-old things come forth. If we refuse to look at these deeper areas of our being, we are running from our true self, refusing to let God meet us in our existential, real self.

Karl Rahner insists strongly on deeper prayer in order that man can enter into freedom.

> No man can give himself the freedom he needs to respond totally to God. For this task he needs to be set free by God Himself, and he is set free only in prayer. Prayer then is the way, because it is the expression of human powerlessness, the affirmation of man's fundamental nothingness and the cutting off of all means of escape. [4]

MYSTICISM—A LONG CHRISTIAN TRADITION

This has been the Christian tradition for the first 16 centuries when mysticism was not feared but was sought for by all who turned within their "hearts" and found God dwelling, ready to heal all who cried out in their inner brokenness to be healed. Interior prayer was of the essence of the Christian, not only communal, shared prayer or liturgical prayer, but most primary — deep, interior prayer. Each Christian knew that he had to go aside and enter into his "inner chamber" (Matt. 6:6) and there adore the Heavenly Father in his heart.

When martyrdom became no longer a common invitation to Christians to surrender themselves for love of Jesus Christ, men and women fled into the physical deserts of Egypt, Syria and Mesopotamia and there they spent their days and nights crying out to the Lord to heal their inner selves, in the deepest part of their consciousness and even their unconscious. They synchronized the healing name of Jesus with their breathing so that the Holy Spirit released a presence of Jesus as Healer and Lord to the individual's consciousness. A text, falsely accredited to St. John Chrysostom, gives the common faith of the early Christians:

> The name of our Lord Jesus Christ, descending into the depths of the heart, will subdue the serpent holding sway over the pastures of the heart and will save our soul and bring it to life. Thus abide constantly with the name of Lord Jesus Christ, so that the heart swallows the Lord and the Lord the heart and the two become one. But this work is not done in one or two days; it needs many years and a long time. For great and prolonged labor is needed to cast out the foe so that Christ dwells in us.

Down through the mystical traditions of the Eastern Fathers of the hesychastic tradition, the apophatic stress of St. Gregory of Nyssa and Pseudo-Dionysius and the Western mystics of St. Augustine, St. Bernard, the 14th century Rhenish and Flemish mystics, the English classic of the *Cloud of Unknowing* and Juliana of Norwich and the 16th century Spanish mystics, St. John of the Cross and St. Teresa of Avila, the common teaching is that man must move beyond the superficial prayer of words only and enter into the deepest reaches of his personality, there to encounter God who calls man into his unique self by the look of His love given in utter silence of man's activity and total surrender to the indwelling Trinity. In a very well described experience, a modern Christian mystic and great scientist, Teilhard de Chardin expresses this universal movement that man must make from his superficial consciousness into his deeper self:

> .. .I took the lamp and, leaving the zone of everyday occupations and relationships where everything seems clear, I went down into my inmost self, to the deep abyss whence I feel dimly that my power of action emanates. But as I moved further and further away from the conventional certainties by which social life is superficially illuminated, I became aware that I was losing contact with myself. At each step of the descent a new person was disclosed within me of whose name I was no longer sure, and who no longer obeyed me. And when I had to stop my exploration because the path faded from beneath my steps, I found a bottomless abyss at my feet, and out of it came—arising I know not from where—the current which I dare to call my life.[5]

Such a form of prayer is hardly occultism! It is the type of prayer that will lead the Christian into a purity of heart in order to see God. It is hardly a technique induced to "reduce their mind to a blank condition and their will to passivity so as to invite supernatural spirits or demons to supply them with many wonderful experiences," to

quote again Watchman Nee.[6] It requires the greatest
discipline and the deepest faith. One has to push himself
into a continued faith-consciousness that God is present
within the desert of his heart, even though there be no
images to hide behind. Stripped of every help but the
"buckler of faith," the Christian stands nude before the
Lord, crying out to Him to come to his rescue.

The humbled Christian knows his creatureliness. He
sees the enemies within himself. His soul is affrighted. He
calls out to the Lord: "For we are bowed in the dust, our
bodies crushed to the ground. Rise! Come to our help!
Redeem us for the sake of Your love" (Ps. 44:25-26).

DEEPER SELF-KNOWLEDGE

If we have the courage to be quiet and relax so as to
descend into the depths of our being in union with Jesus
Christ we begin to see the greater part of our being
submerged below the normal line of controlled consciousness. What we know about our habitual selves is very little
compared to what is hidden beneath. We live in a
controlled knowledge of who we are and who God is and
who our neighbors are. But if we enter this inner world
with faith, we find much darkness. Yet we find that all of
what we are encountering is a vital part of our life
experiences. They are there, with a great potential to be
called into both good and evil. It is here that our greatest
experience in life of death and resurrection into Christ
Jesus takes place.

In the words of St. Gregory of Sinai, "to force our
mind into our heart" is for the Christian to push his
consciousness of the indwelling Lord Jesus and His

immense healing love as a light to illuminate the areas of inner darkness and transform all into a "new creature" in Him.

USE OF TECHNIQUES

The religion of Jesus Christ is incarnational. God became man by taking unto His divine nature a human, material nature. Matter, unlike the teaching of Manicheanism and Platonism, is not created evil. It can, especially since the Incarnation, become a meeting place with the Divine. We cannot, therefore, ignore the material world around us, especially the fact that we are made up of matter. We do not oppose our material bodies as enemies of our souls. We are total beings, bodied, souled and spirited beings.

Throughout the history of Christianity there have been many reform movements that have sought to recall Christians back to a more simple, pristine vision of Christianity and away from an exaggerated attachment to the externals of religion. In the 16th and 17th century there rose up in Europe a puritan protest against Roman Catholicism. Material techniques that had been in use from apostolic times such as sacraments and sacramentals, use of pictures, statues, incense, candles etc. were wiped away from many Christian churches of the Reformation. A simplified return directly to Jesus was advocated that accentuated the theological position that Jesus Christ had done it all; hence there was no need for man to get too involved beyond exercising a deep belief in Jesus Christ as Savior. Only sin and corruption could come from man's nature and the material world.

MATERIAL TECHNIQUES

Yet great damage to the Christian faith results when Christians ignore their bodies in prayer, ignore the use of material techniques that allow them to become integrated, centered more deeply upon the indwelling Trinity. We are using techniques constantly. The charismatic preacher uses techniques in preaching to hold an audience attentive so that his words can sink deeply into their consciousness and move them to a reform of life. The healer imposes hands upon the sick and maimed and these believe that they have experienced once more the healing hands of Jesus Christ.

The Anglicans, Catholics and Orthodox have always maintained a healthy use of material techniques in their prayer-life. Bodily gestures in the Divine Liturgy, the use of bread and wine, oil, holy water, sacraments whereby the minister touches and consecrates a newborn babe into the Christian community, he blesses the spouses, newly ordained priests are consecrated with oil and the imposition of hands, the sick are anointed with oil and imposition of hands, the sinner is absolved and healed by a touch and words of forgiveness.

Should we fear therefore techniques that we can find used by all humans regardless of what country and what religion in order to become quieted? Man universally the world over has learned to quiet his psychic inner world by a rhythmic breathing. The body, soul and spirit merge into a relaxed "whole" person as God's breath is followed inwardly and outwardly, back and forth. One can concentrate on a burning candle and be powerfully aware of Jesus Christ as the light of the world. Or one gazes lovingly at the tabernacle that contains the Blessed Sacrament, at a scene of nature, a picture or statue and he finds a reposeful and deeply prayerful attitude coming over him. Churches have always realized the powerful technique of elevating music in church services to calm the participants and open their deeper selves to prayerful worship.

We note that such techniques are powerful aids to center us and calm our distracted minds and hearts so that we can pray with greater concentration and a fuller consciousness. Such fixation points pull our dispersion to a centering-point so that our hearts can move easily to contemplate the transcendent God as immanently present within us. The ultimate worth of any technique must be measured by the fruit produced. Hence no Christian ought to condemn out of hand any technique, be it yoga, the use of music in prayer, chants, Silva Mind-Control, Arica, T.M. or whatever unless for that person it has not been a help but a definite hindrance to prayer. A technique has no meaning unless we ask the question: "How is it being used? What are the fruits that come from such use? Does it help us or others to pray with greater consciousness, beyond the habitual, superficial level of controlled, discursive prayer?"

The Holy Spirit can touch the human heart and release it for greater prayer and greater healing power from Jesus Christ through any cultural setting, through the use of a great variety of material techniques. The ultimate criterion of whether the Holy Spirit is operating in the lives of Christians or even non-Christians is the sincerity of those persons to encounter God and surrender their lives to His dominance. This sincerity can be measured not by words alone but by deeds. When we see a godly life lived by a person who claims that such and such a technique has helped him to become a better person, we must recognize

that the Spirit of Jesus has met him deeply and transformed his life.

St. Paul gives us the criterion for discerning the
presence of the Holy Spirit through the fruits He produces
in our lives.

> If you are led by the Spirit, no law can touch you. When
> self-indulgence is at work the results are obvious: fornication,
> gross indecency and sexual irresponsibility; idolatry and
> sorcery; feuds and wrangling, jealousy, bad temper and
> quarrels; disagreements, factions, envy; drunkenness, orgies
> and similar things. I warn you now, as I warned you before:
> those who behave like this will not inherit the kingdom of
> God. What the Spirit brings is very different: love, joy, peace,
> patience, kindness, goodness, trustfulness, gentleness and
> self-control. There can be no law against things like that, of
> course (Gal. 5:18-23).

FOOTNOTES

Chapter 1

[1]Cited by Dr. Ira Progoff in his: *Depth Psychology and Modern Man* (N.Y., 1959) pp. 250-251.

[2]A. Gehlen: *Urmensch and Spatkultur* (Bonn, 1956) p. 133.

[3]F. S. C. Northrop: "Man's Relation to the Earth in Its Bearing on His Aesthetic, Ethical and Legal Values" in: *Man's Role in Changing the Face of the Earth*; ed. by Wm. L. Thomas, Jr. and others (Chicago, Ill., 1956) p. 1056.

[4]St. Ignatius to the Ephesians, 15; *Fathers of the Church* Series (Washington, D.C., 1946) p. 93.

Chapter 2

[1]J. Macquarrie: *Principles of Christian Theology* (London, 1966) pp. VII, 1,3,8 ss.

[2]Cited in: *The Art of Prayer*, compiled by Igumen Chariton, tr. by E. Kadloubovsky and E. M. Palmer (London, 1966) pp. 190-191.

[3]J. Macquarrie:*Principles of Christian Theology* (London, 1966) pp. 230 ss.; 249-398.

[4]Cf. the New Jerusalem Bible (N.Y., 1966) p. 147, ftnote n.

[5]*Mystic Treatises* by Isaac of Nineveh; tr. by A. J. Wensinck (Amsterdam, 1923) p. 8.

[6]Apophthegmata Patrum; PG. 65, 88.

[7]Gregory of Nyssa: on Virginity; PG. 46, 352A-D, cited in: *From Glory to Glory* ed. by J. Danielou and H. Musurillo (N.Y., 1961) pp. 102-3.

[8]Thomas Merton: The Climate of Monastic Prayer (Spencer, Mass., 1969) p. 128.

[9]Karl Rahner: *Everyday Faith* (N.Y., 1968) p. 112.

Chapter 3

[1]See the chapter on the Jesus prayer in my work: *The Breath of the Mystic* (Denville, N.J., 1974) pp. 83-107.

[2]*The Art of Prayer*, compiled by Igumen Chariton of Valamo (London, 1966) p. 17.

[3]*The Art of Prayer*, p. 86.

[4]*The Art of Prayer*, p. 115.

[5]*The Way of a Pilgrim* and *The Pilgrim Continues His Way*, tr. from the Russian by R. M. French (N.Y. 2nd ed., 1952).

[6]*Op. cit., The Art of Prayer*, p. 35.

[7]J. D. Salinger, *Franny and Zooey* (New York, 1955), p. 164.

Chapter 4

[1]St. Macarius of Egypt: Hom. Spir. XXXIII: PG..XXXIV: 741 ss.

[2]St. Antony: *Directions on Life in Christ*, in: *Early Fathers from the Philokalia*; tr. by E. Kadloubovsky and G. E. Palmer (London, 1954) p. 43.

[3]St. Gregory of Nyssa: *De Anima et Resurrectionis*, in: *Library of Nicene and Post-Nicene Fathers*; p. 450.

Chapter 5

[1]*The Art of Prayer, op. cit.*, pp. 45-46.

[2]PG. 34; 658.

Chapter 6

[1]G. A. Maloney, S.J.: *The Breath of the Mystic* (Denville, N.J., 1974) p. 42.

[2]I am indebted for much of this material to Father Irénée Hausherr, S.J.: *Hesychasme et Priere* (Rome, 1966).

[3]St. Augustine: *Epist. Class.* III, 121; *Patrologia Latina* (PL) 33;493-507.

[4]St. Basil: *Reg. fus. tr.: Patrologia Graeca* 31 (P.G.; Migne) 920C-921B.

[5]*Ibid, Regula 5.*

[6]Hesychius: *Century II*; PG. 93, 1513B (7).

[7]St. Basil: *In Julittam* 4; PG. 32;245A.

Chapter 7

[1]These are Heidegger's terms or concepts as used by Dr. John Macquarrie. Cf: Studies in *Christian Existentialism* (London, 1965) and his *God-Talk: An Examination of the Language and Logic of Theology* (London, 1967).

[2]J. Macquarrie, *God-Talk*, p. 80.

[3]See fuller text in: George A. Maloney, S.J.: *Mystic of Fire and Light: St. Symeon the New Theologian* (Denville, N.J., 1975) pp. 125-127.

[4]B. Lonergan: *Method in Theology* (N.Y., 1967) p. 107.

[5]John C. Lilly: *The Center of the Cyclone* (N.Y., 1972) p. 196.

[6]Nicetas Stethatos: *Century, I*; Migne: PG. 120, Ch. 70, 884B.

[7]John Climacus: Gradus 7 of his *Scalae Perfectionis*, PG. 88, 816.

[8]*Ustav* (Rule) of Nil Sorsky. I cite from the critical edition of Borovkova-Maikova, M.A.: "Nila Sorskago Predanie i Ustav s vstupitel'noi stat'ei found in: *Pamiatniki drevnei pis'mennosti*, Gradus 7, PG. 88, 808C; also 805D.

[9]Evagrius: *De Oratione*, PG. 79, #5, 1168D.

[10]As cited by Nil Sorsky in his *Ustav*, p. 73.

[11]Isaac the Syrian: found in *Dobrotolubie*, the Slavonic translation of the *Philokalia*, ed. by Bishop Theophan the Recluse; T. II (Moscow, 1884; ed. 2) #219, pp. 775-776.

[12]Isaac, *ibid.*

[13]Isaac, *ibid.*

[14]Cf. Evagrius, *De Oratione, op. cit.*#7, 1169A; #8, 1169B.

[15]Symeon the New Theologian; PG. 120, 490A. See also Cassian's doctrine on not forcing tears: *Conferences*, IX, Ch. 30, in: *Sources Chrétiennes*, Vol. 54; Bk. VIII-XVII (Paris, 1958) pp. 65-66.

[16]Cited in Nil Sorsky's *Ustav, op. cit.* p. 73.

[17]St. Gregory Nyssa: *De Beatitudine*, III, PG. 44, 1224C.

[18]Isaac: Logos 75; ed. cit. p. 508.

[19]Ephraem the Syrian: *Sermo asceticus*; ed. Assemani; Vol. 1, p. 61.

[20]Symeon the New Theologian; PG. 120, 640D; 645B; 517D.

[21]Climacus, *Gradus 7*, 804B. Cf. John Damascene: *De Fide Orthodoxa*, PG. 94, 1124C.

[22]Cited from Nil's *Ustav*, p. 78.

[23]*Life of Antony* in: Post-Nicene Fathers, 2nd Ser. 4 (Grand Rapids, 1957) p. 214.

[24]Symeon the New Theologian: *Practical and Theological Precepts*,

in: *Writings From the Philokalia on Prayer of the Heart*; tr. by E. Kadloubovsky and G. Palmer (Faber & Faber, London) p. 113.

[25] This same phenomenon is attested in the life of St. Ignatius of Loyola as he records in his autobiography that he wept continually for two years from 1540 to 1542.

[26] Isaac the Syrian: *Directions on Spiritual Training*, in: *Early Fathers From the Philokalia*; tr. by E. Kadloubovsky and G. Palmer (Faber & Faber, London), pp. 251-252.

[27] Climacus, *Gradus 7, op. cit.* 816B.

Chapter 9

[1] V. E. Frankl: *La psychotherapie et son image de l'homme* (Paris, 1970) p. 150.

[2] *Ibid.* p. 152.

[3] Rudolf Otto: *Mysticism East and West*; tr. B. Bracey and R. Payne (N.Y., 1932) pp. 150-1.

[4] Carl Rogers: *On Becoming a Person* (Boston, 1970) p. 90.

[5] Carl Jung: *Modern Man in Search of a Soul* (N.Y., 1933) p. 259.

[6] N. Kazantzakis: *Report to Greco* (N.Y., 1958) pp. 279-280.

[7] Quoted in *Soul Afire*; ed. H. A. Reinhold (Garden City, N.Y., 1973) p. 449.

[8] *The Cloud of Unknowing*; chap. 34.

[9] Ira Progoff: *The Cloud of Unknowing* (N.Y., 1957) p. 34.

[10] *Ibid.* p. 34.

[11] *The Cloud*, ch. 8.

[12] Carlos Castaneda: *A Separate Reality* (N.Y., 1971) p. 43.

[13]K. Wapnick: "Mysticism and Schizophrenia," in: *The Highest State of Consciousness*; ed. by John White (Garden City, N.Y., 1971) p. 172.

[14]Paul Tillich: *The Courage To Be* (Boston, Mass., 1952) pp. 39-66.

[15] St. John of the Cross: Ascent of Mount Carmel; ed. and trans. by E. Allison Peers (Garden City, N.Y., 1958) II,XI; p. 119.

[16]*Ascent* II,XI; p. 121.

Chapter 10

[1]T. Merton: *Conjectures of a Guilty Bystander* (Garden City, N.Y., 1965) pp. 141-142.

[2]T. Merton: *Contemplation in a World of Action* (Garden City, N.Y., 1971) p. 54.

[3]St. Basil: *Homily 12*, 4; PG. 31;393.

[4]St. Ambrose: *Expositio in Psalmum CXVIII*, 8th Sermon, 22; *PL.* 15;1503.

[5]*The Didache*; in: *Ancient Christian Writers*; ed. J. Quasten & J. Plumpe; tr. by J. A. Kleist, (Baltimore, Md., 1967) Vol. 6; p. 17.

[6]St. Ambrose: *Naboth the Poor Man*; *PL.* 14,12,53; p. 747.

[7]St. Basil: *Homily 6 against riches*, 7; PG. 31; 277.

[8]*The Teachings of Pope Paul VI* (Washington, D.C., 1972) p. 384.

Chapter 11

[1]Norman Pittenger: *Process Thought and Christian Faith* (N.Y., 1968) p. 13.

[2]V. Lossky: *The Mystical Theology of the Eastern Church* (Cambridge & London, 1973) p. 67.

[3]*Future of Man* (London & N.Y., 1964) pp. 307-308.

[4]Emile Rideau: *The Thought of Teilhard de Chardin*; tr. by Rene Hague (New York & Evanston, 1967) p. 185.

[5]*Phenomenon of Man*; tr. by Bernard Wall (New York, 1959) p. 288.

[6]*Ibid.*, p. 288.

[7]C. S. Lewis: *The Great Divorce* (New York, 1946) p. 128.

[8]Piet Schoonenberg, S.J.: "I Believe in Eternal Life" *Concilium, Dogma, the Problem of Eschatology* (N.Y.–Glen Rock, N.J., 1969) p. 110.

[9]Origen, *On First Principles*; tr. and ed. by G. W. Butterworth, (N.Y., 1966) p. 248.

[10]Hans Lietzmann: *A History of the Early Church* (N.Y., 1961) Vol. 2, p. 310.

[11]*On Perfection*; tr. by V. W. Callahan *Ascetical Works*; *Fathers of the Church*; Vol. 58 (Washington, D.C., 1967) p. 122.

[12]*Life of Moses, From Glory to Glory*; tr. and ed. by J. Danielou and H. Musurillo (N.Y., 1961) p. 144.

[13]*Ibid.*

[14]*Canticle of Canticles, From Glory. . .op. cit.*, p. 270.

[15]*Ibid.*

[16]Prolegomena to *Library of Nicene and Post-Nicene Fathers*, Series 2; Vol. 5 (Grand Rapids, 1952) p. 15.

[17]*De anima et resurrectione*; tr. by V. W. Callahan, *The Father of the Church*; Vol. 58 (Washington, D.C., 1967) pp. 241-242.

[18]Cf. Karl Rahner, *On the Theology of Death* (N.Y., 1961) pp. 21-39.

[19]Paul Chauchard, *Man and Cosmos* (N.Y., 1965); tr. by George Courtright, p. 143.

[20]Cf. also: Jose-Maria Gonzalez-Ruiz, "Should We De-Mythologize the 'Separated Soul?'," *Concilium*; Vol. 41, *Dogma, the Problem of Eschatology* (N.Y.–Glen Rock, N.J., 1969) pp. 82-96; also Anton Grabner-Haider, "The Biblical Understanding of 'Resurrection' and 'Glorification,' " *ibid.*, pp. 66-81.

[21]Sermon 242, c.3, n.5; *PL.* 38;1140).

[22]Spirit. Cant. Stan. 8, n.3, Peers, II, p. 229.

[23]I am indebted in this section to the insights of John A. T. Robinson in his work, *In the End, God...* (London, 1950) pp. 99-128.

[24]Cited by Robinson, *op. cit.*, p. 115.

[25]*Ibid.*, p. 123.

[26]*Ibid.*, pp. 122-123.

[27]St. Augustine: *De Civitate Dei*, 21,26,2 and *Enchir.* 69, cited by J. N. D. Kelly: *Early Christian Doctrines* (N.Y., 1959) p. 485.

[28]St. Gregory of Nyssa: *Life of Moses*; PG. 44, 405D, cited from *From Glory to Glory*; ed. Jean Danielou and H. Musurillo (N.Y., 1961) p. 150.

[29]H. Urs von Balthasar: *Le chrétien Bernanos* (Paris, 1963) pp. 160-161.

Appendix

[1]Watchman Nee: *The Spiritual Man*; Vol. 3 (N.Y., 1968) p. 26 ss.

[2]Ira Progoff: *Jung's Psychology and Its Social Meaning*; (N.Y., 1955) p. 66.

[3]Erich Fromm: *Zen Buddhism and Psychoanalysis* (N.Y., 1960) p. 97.

[4]Karl Rahner: *On Prayer*, (N.Y., 1968) p. 15.

[5]P. Teilhard de Chardin: *The Divine Milieu*, (N.Y., 1960) p. 48.

[6]Watchman Nee: *op. cit.*, p. 26.